The Caring Parent

The
Caring Parent

Answers to Questions About Children

Paul D. Warner

Bookcraft
Salt Lake City, Utah

Library of Congress Catalog Card Number: 84-71990
ISBN 0-88494-535-9

First Printing, 1984

Lithographed in the United States of America
PUBLISHERS PRESS
Salt Lake City, Utah

For Sherry
and for my teachers
Kristin, Jennifer, David, and Lori

Contents

Some Basic Principles   1

How presumptuous of me even to consider writing a book like this! To pretend that I have the one right answer to all the questions which have bedeviled parents since Adam and Eve, the one way to solve all our children's problems, is pure gall. In truth, there may be a hundred different, equally valid approaches to each question raised in this book. In my own defense, though, I am writing it to share my philosophy of child rearing, which to me is credible or I wouldn't be writing about it. I hope that as you read the responses I give to the child-management questions which typically arise in my practice, you will develop your own philosophy for governing your own children. I have tried to highlight what in my experience are the most important principles of child management. More important, I have attempted to present ideas for working with your own children by giving you glimpses of actual problems I have seen in other families and then suggesting specific strategies for dealing with those problems.

The question-answer format helps to get directly at several typical problems in raising children.

Before I start responding to questions, I want to lay a foundation of general principles for sound child management. Please read carefully the following section because everything that follows is built on this foundation. If you attempt to implement the strategies suggested in this book without these fundamental principles in mind, you will likely fail.

Parents, Get Your Act Together

As father and mother, you cannot effectively manage your home without first agreeing on what it is you are trying to accomplish as a family. What do you want your family and home to be like? This does not mean what your neighbors expect of your family, but what *you* desire as a *couple*. First of all, talk this over together as long as is necessary to establish agreement. This agreement results in parental unity, a crucial principle in rearing children successfully. Parental unity precedes everything else, since you can't plan a journey until you agree on the destination.

You probably assume that you already have a consensus on family objectives, but even the best teams don't achieve unity of purpose until they have specifically plotted out their response to the variety of issues that affect all families *and have come to agreement on them.* Recently I was assured by a young couple that they were in harmony about the organization of their home. They were a little annoyed when I asked what time they had decided that their children should be in bed. The mother said "seven o'clock" at the same moment the father admitted, "We don't set a time." After a nervous giggle and a look at each other, they agreed they had some discussing to do.

If you find yourselves in complete agreement on all of the large issues you discuss, there may be a question about whether you are being "up front" with each other. Honest agreement without lengthy negotiation is rarely achieved. In truly frank interchange, most couples find several areas where there is not much common ground. Presumably you both have convictions about what a good home should be like, but it is perfectly natural to disagree about *means* (how to accomplish goals) rather than *ends*. Concern for your partner's point of view will allow room for compromise if you are each willing to listen to the other and assume a reasonable attitude about your ability to accomplish your family needs.

Keep the immediate object in mind: unity. Then look for compromise. For example, it is not as important that you agree on the "ideal" or "right" bedtime as it is that you both agree on some time. I find that often parents have not agreed about even the simplest matters, such as whether it is okay for the children to play outside later than 6:00 P.M. Maybe you, Dad, feel your child should be free to play outdoors late in the evening as you did when you were a boy; whereas you, Mom, worry about the children's safety and want them in early. In such a case, you may both be right and both be wrong, but what's right or wrong is not the real issue here: only conversion or compromise can bring unity, and usually it turns out to be the latter.

Incidentally, you should try to avoid disagreement over "right" and "wrong" ways to manage your children. There is no evidence that children who finish play at six and go to bed at seven are better off physically, emotionally, or mentally than those who keep later hours—or vice versa. It is simply a matter of what fits your particular family.

Within your "particular" family, you have "particular" children—that is, in your family, each member is unique. So when you have reached agreement on the management of your family life, begin talking about the needs of each individual child. Discuss the strengths and weaknesses of each. Perhaps your oldest child reads well, thinks clearly and logically, and does highly creative things. On the other hand, does he lack other skills? Does he fail to express his feelings openly? Does he withdraw in the face of frustration? Is he in reasonable control of his emotions? Is he at the appropriate maturity level? Try to agree about the specific needs of your child, then make a plan which will help him build on his strengths and practice away his weaknesses. Do this for each child.

Unless you can come to agreement on the details of family living and the specific needs of each of your children, any management program you begin will be in jeopardy. Your lack of agreement will create inconsistencies in what you expect of each other and of your children. It will confuse your children and increase the likelihood that they simply will not do what you want. Most children are quick to pick up inconsistencies and disagreement between parents and may pit one parent against the other. Without unity, you cannot train the child to be responsible to a specific set of principles consistently administered in your home. Clearly, then, this agreement is the first step in managing your family, the starting place for family improvement and growth.

Keep Your Cool

What is the climate of your home like? Is it sunny, stormy, intermittent clouds, or "travelers' advisory"? The atmosphere in any family is created by the parents, and the stability of the home depends on its emotional climate. It is our job as parents to create more sunny than stormy days. Do we know what kind of climate we're modeling?

When we are out of emotional control, we present our children with a model which encourages them to lose control in turn, and this can become the catalyst for a chaotic atmosphere at home. If we cannot control *our* emotions, we cannot expect our children to control theirs. When we practice emotional self-control, the tension level in the family will drop. Those things that typically upset us, like gum on the living-room carpet, drips on the sofa, and fights over TV programs, do not have to send us into a frenzy. How many of us react to spilled milk as we would to a broken leg? Reducing our own anxiety at the moment of crisis puts us in a much better position to implement fair, non-destructive consequences in a more consistent manner. When our emotions erupt, we simply lessen our effectiveness. Eruption usually leads to overdisciplining. Sometimes we build up layers of frustration throughout the day, and when our pile of frustration is deep enough, the slightest spark can cause an explosion.

The answer? A deliberate decision to be calm in the face of upsets. Calmness—this is the factor that can change the home forecast from cloudy to sunny.

I once knew a father whose oldest son had taken up the drums and practiced incessantly day in and day out. The father finally couldn't take it any longer. In a breakdown of self-control, he kicked a hole in the bass drum, saying, "Stop playing those drums or I am going to go crazy!" Of course the son stopped, and it wasn't long before both Mom and Dad realized that their son had stopped playing the drums altogether. It's hard to blame him.

In calmness, we can take stock of the real conditions

around us and respond without creating a tense home environment. I remember explaining this concept to a middle-aged couple in my office; the very aloof father grinned. He was great at keeping calm. In fact he'd been doing too well! He had to learn that practicing calmness and concealing our emotions are not the same thing.

Calmness means talking out our feelings rather than acting them out. Emotional calmness does not mean that we put a lid on our emotions and repress them. On the contrary, it means that we learn to express our emotions calmly, while we are experiencing them. If we feel frustrated, those frustrations should be talked as they occur, rather than held in a large bucket of frustration that spills over in tirades against our children. Yes, I'm suggesting that when we feel irritated at our children's behavior, we should express it to them. The unacceptable behavior should be discussed, but the child should still feel loved.

"Talking feelings out" means talking with someone about our feelings until they aren't a concern any longer. When we talk about our emotions, we should always remember to use the personal *I* and leave *you* out of the dialogue. If we are projecting blame or criticizing someone in an attempt to eliminate our own anxieties, we are only going to create resistance and defensiveness on the part of the other person who, typically, will tune us out.

Emotional calmness also implies keeping our jets cool even at the height of the crisis, instead of firing our rockets over every mishap. We act, we don't react. This will help us stay one step ahead of our children and keep us there. It allows our children to see us as models for handling emotional disturbance in a positive way.

They see us talking our feelings out instead of acting them out. When we are angry, we yell, scream, or hit the wall; we must teach our children the exact opposite if we wish them to develop productively. I will never forget the mother who threw a tantrum in my office because her little girl would not sit still and pay attention. The mother's tantrum wouldn't have alarmed me so much if she hadn't come into therapy to get help for her daughter's tantrums.

In addition, emotional calmness allows for new dialogue in the home. When we respond calmly to things that typically set parents off, we find it easier to talk to our children about what we expect of them, rather than what we want them to stop doing. Unfortunately, most of us wait until catastrophes happen and then try to stop them. Instead, we must create a calm style of training in our homes to direct our children toward our designated goals for them.

How to do this? If you have decided that your children need to learn to talk instead of fight, you can interrupt their fighting by ordering them to stop. But it's more effective to emphasize the thing that you want them to do. Instead of shouting, "Stop it," say, "I want you children to talk differently to each other. Think of ways in which you could handle this problem without fighting so you live the family rule of talking out your differences." The simple alternative of giving positive direction will clarify in your child's mind your expectations and will increase the likelihood that he will live by them.

Many of us expend much energy telling our children what *not* to do. A child's mind has a difficult time with the idea of "not doing" something. It is like asking a person to imagine a man not painting a house. On the other hand, it is very easy for us to imagine a man painting a house. Getting things going is easy to do if we practice giving two-part instructions to our children when disciplining them. First, tell them what to stop doing and, second, what to *start* doing. "Stop fighting and please cooperate." This step sounds too simple, but it can have a profound effect on the climate of the home.

Everyone has times of tension and stress, so it is important to develop the ability to relax. We all relax in different ways. As a parent, you need to remember to relax and do more of it. Reducing tension in your home begins by reducing tension in your own life. A good place to begin—learn to laugh more. Daily exercise reduces mental as well as physical tension, helping us to cope with stress. It burns off tension. If we learn also to exercise the spirit, we strengthen our ability to face stressful situations.

We should also learn to relax as a family. There are very few kids who can stay tense when playing simple, enjoyable games together with their family, especially with Mom and Dad. Rhythm games, "Simon Says," and body-movement games of all types are good activities for young children who seem tense. I like the effect of good music on my inner self and the very positive influence it seems to have on my children.

Mind relaxation can be very helpful. The children should sit or lie in a very comfortable place. Ask them to imagine certain fantasies that are relaxing, such as lying on a beach with a bird singing in a tree, the waves and the ocean gently flowing onto the sand, and the sun shining down. Our children from time to time need to have a quiet place and quiet moments. It would be beneficial to set aside a place at home where children can go to do their quiet things and be alone.

These are only a few suggestions, and you can probably think of many others, such as family-group reading, family walks—anything that can disarm states of tension.

Rules for the Home

After outlining our family goals and deciding to face all stressful conditions with calmness, we must begin to establish clear and easily understood rules. These rules should reflect the development level and perceived needs of each child. I suggest two types of rules: family rules and individual rules. It is important to remember to derive rules from the goals previously identified.

"Family rules" could include no fighting, making beds, cleaning rooms each day, respecting self and others, and talking politely. Such general rules pertain to family living and apply to all members of the family. They should be specific and few in number.

Individual rules have to do with the perceived needs of your individual children. If one of your children, for example, needs to learn to share, you may establish a rule specifically for him that suggests "we share our toys and belongings." There is great power in the clear statement of a rule to a child.

In many cases, you will notice remarkable growth and development in your children by merely stating the rule you want them to follow. As your children respond to this new "goal," you will be delighted to see how often you will not even have to worry about consequences to get them to live their new rule. I have seen many children delight in the mere fact that as parents we have enough interest and have taken enough time to think through what it is we expect of them. Often this is enough for your children to begin to change. These rules should be "do" rules and not "don't do" rules.

Good rules imply movement toward some goal. A "no fighting rule," for example, should require a cooperative sharing behavior. Furthermore, we should not only *encourage* desired behavior, but insist that our children *practice* it until they are doing what we expect. In this case, the chances of our children moving toward their goals are increased.

If one rule is good, then fifty must be even better — right? Wrong! Rules should be few in number, specific, and easy to understand. Some families have long lists of rules. One mother told me that she really believed in rules and had a list of them to prove it. Reading through the list, she was puzzled by one rule. After a minute she looked up and said, "Golly, I'd forgotten we had this rule, and it's so good too." The problem with having too many rules is that neither Mom, Dad, nor the kids can remember them all. This is a sure guarantee of failure.

When developing rules for your family, it is important that each of your children feel some involvement in the process. At some point, sit down with your children and discuss how they want to be involved in the family and how they think the family should be functioning. Before you establish rules for an individual or the family, you should solicit the ideas of your children and take their suggestions into account.

When you develop rules, it is also important not to assume that your children will understand what you expect of them if you just make a chart or mention the rule in passing. You should bring each family member in separately, then collectively, and very specifically explain the new pattern of behavior. The explanation should clarify where the family is going. The father might state the new rules and lead out in the discussion, while Mother repeats what Father has said. Then each child should explain what he thought he heard to make sure that everyone understands very clearly what is expected. Then you are ready to move on to the next step.

Training Your Children Rather Than Punishing Them

Whether you want to be or not, you are a teacher. In fact, your role as parent could be most accurately described as that of an educator. Up to 90 percent of what your children become is molded in the home. Do you know what you're teaching your children, and more important, do you know that you *can* teach?

Right after I was asked to join the faculty at Brigham Young University, I had one night of near hysteria. I couldn't think of anything to teach my students. I felt I had some knowledge but wasn't sure how to present it. However, much of my panic subsided when I found out the specific courses that I would be teaching. When I entered class that first day, I was almost confident. Looking back, I realize that my confidence came from knowing what I was going to teach, having a clear set of objectives in mind for my students and, at some level, a *plan of attack* for meeting those challenges. I found after several months of teaching that my style was different from that of other professors, but my students were learning.

As a parent, I'm learning that I can teach my kids almost any skill if I have a plan and will try to understand their needs, set some clear goals, and then teach. For me, it's nothing more than giving my children opportunities to practice the behavior or skill I want them to acquire.

Recently, my wife and I realized the need to help our five-year-old son become more tidy and to pick up after himself. He's now very proud of his new semi-official title: "A great boy who's learning to pick his things up." When it's time to remind him to collect his things, my wife will say, "David, I want you to come and practice

picking up. Look, Dad, how well David's learning to
pick up. He's getting better and better." David takes real
pride in learning a skill which seems important to Mom
and Dad. This is the real secret to training. What we ask
children to do must have some importance, and we must
show them how to perform the task and then reassure
them that they can do it. When you develop a rule in
your family that says, "We make our own beds and clean
our rooms," remember to train your children how to
comply. You may assume that your children automatically acquire the skills to clean their rooms, but this is not
the case. Even with older children, it is best to spend
whatever time it takes to teach them how to perform the
task. If our rule is to talk things over rather than fight,
then we should role-play or demonstrate how to practice
cooperative behavior until we feel satisfied that they
have it down pat.

Training is the key to effective discipline. Training
implies gentle and consistent persuasiveness, not punishment. It implies that you as parents approach the problems of discipline with the attitude that you are moving
your children toward positive goals, that they have the
ability to be trained, and that you will spend the
necessary time to train them in what they are supposed
to do. Training is a journey: it takes time and lasts as
long as your children live at home.

To train effectively you must give your time and
overcome the tendency to discipline from a distance.
Observe how often you shout across a room or yell at
your children down the hall. Effective discipline requires
that you move toward your child, get his attention calmly, explain very clearly what it is you want him to do,
and model or practice that behavior until the child understands and complies. In some cases, a child will not feel

motivated enough to practice what parents expect; in those cases, consequences must be defined and applied.

Applying Consequences

If your child decides that he is not able to live the family rule or is not willing to be trained, it becomes necessary to apply a little gentle force in the form of appropriate consequences. Consequences help our children to work toward a positive goal and should not be viewed as a punishment.

You may find it productive to withhold certain of your child's privileges while he practices what he should be doing. If, for example, your child is consistently fighting instead of talking, he may lose some privileges until he has clearly demonstrated compliance; then restore them as reinforcement for living by the family rules.

Be sure to assign specific consequences for the infraction of specific rules. For example, if your child fights, apply a predetermined consequence, such as working cooperatively with the person he fights with and do this consistently for a period of time until you feel satisfied that your child has learned what you expect of him. Using a consequence such as having them pick up trash from the yard with one garbage bag can get them to work together and require cooperative interactions.

If your child misbehaves, it may mean that he has not had enough training. It does not necessarily mean that he is a terrible, vicious person in need of punishment and ridicule. This more positive, directional philosophy allows you to view your child not as a rebel who deliberately misbehaves to get negative attention or to punish you, but as a learner who needs teaching.

Once a child begins to understand this notion, he also begins to see his brothers and sisters as learners too. Not long ago, my daughter ran in to tattle that her younger brother was throwing chocolate papers on our light-colored living-room carpet. She knew the family rule that we "respect self and others," including family property. I suggested to my little tattler that her little brother might not know how to keep the living room clean, and asked her what she thought we could do to help him learn. She said, "I know, Daddy—I can *show* him how." At that point she ran into the living room and said, "See, David, you pick this paper up, and you pick this paper up, and you pick this paper up." Clearly, she had understood that all family members are learners who can be helped by teaching. She became a *teacher* to her younger brother, not just a tattle-tale.

It's much nicer being a learner than a misbehaver. Help your children understand that the application of consequences is not punishment, but rather a chance to practice the right behavior. Remember to reward them for trying. Appropriate consequences allow our children to develop enough motivation to want to change. They also relieve parents of the need to apply physical punishment, which has so many negative by-products.

Anticipating Your Child's Needs
Several Months in Advance

Caring parents should become sensitive to the future needs of their children. If you have a child entering kindergarten a year from now, you can begin to assess what he will need to be able to do in order to succeed in kindergarten. Ask yourself questions: "Does he have the ability to follow simple rules?" "Is he able to cooperate with other children?" As you ponder the challenges facing your child in the months ahead, you can begin to develop rules and expectations that will help him develop those qualities that will allow him to succeed.

Key Concepts

Finally, keep ever in mind the following key concepts:

1. Never use labels like *liar, thief, stealer, sissy.* They can brand a child for life.

2. Be clear about what you want your child to be doing. Avoid getting your child to stop doing something—get him to start doing the thing he needs to do to grow.

3. Tell your child what you are trying to get him to do differently. Goals for your children shouldn't be kept a parents' secret.

4. How is your child unique? What is his special genius? Look for it, uncover it, talk about it.

5. Problem behaviors never belong to one person only; they belong to the family.

6. Blamers try to assess blame. Teach respect, not blaming.

7. All problem behaviors have a cause, a goal, and an outcome. Learn to know what happened, why, and what followed.

8. When parents try to manage behavior, they become part of the dynamic of the problem. Your involvement is as much a part of the situation as your child's.

9. Children need rules but have a difficult time following them consistently. If your child is an exception, you should begin to worry!

10. Values clarify after adolescence. Values are being tested during teenage years.

11.   Teenagers need a lot of explanation for requests made of them. At this stage of life they are hung up on democratic processes.

12.   Parents should have their heads together and find as much agreement about what is right for their home as possible.

13.   Parents who don't agree on what their home and children should be like are probably terribly frustrated by their lack of discipline power.

14.   The most important ingredient in a successful home is *calmness.*

15.   Calmness means talking out emotions, not acting them out.

16.   Calmness doesn't mean avoiding our emotions.

17.   Self-image needs at least three things in order to grow:
      a.   Talking and understanding;
      b.   Positive self-talk;
      c.   Doing good things with recognition.

18.   We should parent with the goal in mind of helping our children learn independence. Letting children go is an essential part of this process.

19.   Parents need their partners. Children need to see their parents as partners.

20.   Total capitulation of your opinion would be better than never agreeing with your partner on a point of discipline.

21.   Parents can try to be consistent but should remember that total consistency is impossible.

22.   Kids need permission to be unpredictable, and parents need permission to change their minds.

23.   Parents aren't always right and shouldn't have to be. Kids aren't always wrong.

24. Most pre-teenage females need strong male figures in their lives to work through their own identities. The same is true for males.

Summary

In this introductory chapter I have tried to present the essentials of effective family management. These principles are not intended as a cookbook approach but rather as guidelines to help modify your unique family into a successful one. Your plan will differ from your neighbor's; but if both families apply these principles, both plans will work.

The important thing is to get started. Begin by coming to agreement on family goals; by learning to be calm; by establishing rules that reflect the development of personality characteristics appropriate for each child and for the family; and by training instead of punishing. Apply pre-established consequences when children are unwilling to live by the rules, and anticipate the needs of your children several months in advance. Neglecting any of these principles will diminish your chances for success. My responses to the questions in the following chapters should be viewed within the framework of principles outlined in this chapter.

Selfishness 2

Question

I have recently become concerned with my seven-year-old daughter's selfishness. I can't remember observing any caring for her brothers, sisters, or anything else for that matter, without some selfish motive behind the act. Sometimes she seems very insensitive to the feelings of others. She seems to be a dissatisfied "pig" always demanding more. Sharing her possessions is out of the question unless my husband and I get on her case about it. I am worried that she will never learn to give of herself to those she should share with and that she will always be a self-centered, selfish person. Is there anything that I can do to help her become more caring?

Answer

First of all, it is important to understand how her self-centeredness differs from that of older children. Egocentricity is natural to this particular phase of her life. Between the ages of two and seven children go through a developmental stage referred to by Piaget as the "pre-operational" period. During this time, a child goes from functioning at a physical or sensory-motor basis to dealing with more symbolic representations of reality. The most obvious feature of this period is the development of language, but another is egocentrism.

Children during this period seem unable to understand or even imagine viewpoints other than their own. At this age they have a difficult time recognizing others' conclusions or perceptions as real. Their logic preempts entertaining anyone else's point of view. At this level your child's morality is very self-centered. If you say to your child, "How would you like it if someone did that to you?" he has a difficult time putting himself in the position of another because he cannot operationalize or understand another's point of view. Piaget in his work found that if a child sees a model of a town or a village from the north, he is unable to imagine what the same town might look like from the south. During this period, you must not expect to reason your child out of her self-centeredness. Reason alone won't teach your child what experience will. She must overcome selfishness through trial and error.

In the case of your daughter, then, her self-centeredness is a normal attribute of this particular time of life. If the behavior persists beyond about age seven, then there are some specific things you can do to help her to grow up or become more concerned about the feelings of others.

In order to help your daughter grow out of her self-orientation, begin by setting rules of fairness in the home. A simple rule such as "We treat ourselves and others fairly" seems to be helpful. Then you can create opportunities for her to practice fairness, such as sharing of duties within the home. She should gradually get the point. Even though your daughter may protest, if you continue to explain that you are trying to be fair and that each must share, she will begin to see herself as a part of a family rather than an isolated entity. This will help her to become less self-oriented.

The second thing to do as your child matures is to create an opportunity for her to examine points of view other than her own, not through lectures, giving advice, teaching, or moralizing, but by asking penetrating questions while listening to her talk. As she talks, even if her point of view is completely wrong, reflect and empathize, by telling her what you heard her say. Reflecting back *her* own point of view will allow her to listen to her own point of view. Many children will argue with themselves and thereby discover a broader perception of the pros and cons of an issue. This is the best way to get them to understand another viewpoint.

Third, try to teach your daughter to empathize with those around her. To teach empathy you must model it. That means that you become a good listener and learn to help your children feel understood. At the same time, if your daughter does not listen to you, you may want to stop and comment that *you* don't feel listened to. Make eye contact, ask her not to interrupt you, and then ask her to parrot back what she thinks she has heard you say. Some parents become very skilled in helping their children not only to listen to words, but to feel the emotion behind the words. This is true empathy. If you can accomplish this with your daughter, she will make great strides toward empathizing with others.

Fourth, I suggest that you establish a simple rule for sharing. A teacher I know made a rule that during recess every member of the class was to find out something positive about someone in the class. In other words, they would find some good thing in another person that they could share with the class when they came in from recess. She called it positive tattling. Each day she devoted some time to positive tattling, when a child would report catching another doing something good. This special kind of awareness helps children to get outside of themselves and begin to appreciate the qualities of others. This is the opposite of egocentrism and helps children become less selfish. A rule in our homes like "We respect self and others" has the same effect.

Fifth, do some special things for your daughter without being asked. If your daughter is continually setting you up to do things for her, you may want to find times when she is not being selfish and do something just for her; if you're not complimented or given appropriate thanks for your thoughtfulness, you may during a quiet moment talk about what is happening in your relationship, particularly in the area of giving and sharing. You may suggest that she is not sharing as much as you'd like, and help her learn to watch for times when others are making special efforts to share with her. She may even need to role play complimenting others before she does it in earnest. Any time your daughter voluntarily shares as you've asked, she should be reinforced in the most positive way. Typically, a hug or a positive comment or praise regarding a voluntary behavior will go a long way in helping her learn to be more giving.

Sixth, since this is a transitional period for your daughter, a time when egocentrism is expected behavior, remember that it will pass. This is a good time for you to learn to be patient. As she matures, particularly between the ages of eight and sixteen, she will become more sensitive to others' needs.

There is a positive side to her self-centeredness: she may be learning to insulate herself from the demanding pressures others will apply on her during adolescence. Perhaps she will be less influenced by those around her. When this insulation is carried to an extreme it may become a problem; but for the most part, self-reliance can be helpful later on. My recommendation is that you learn patience and tolerance of this particular behavior within the guidelines I have mentioned, and she should grow her way out of this problem.

Tantrums 3

Question

My four-year-old daughter throws the meanest tantrums I have ever seen. She begins by asking for something she knows she cannot have. When I refuse her, she begins to whine. I have tried to ignore the whining, but she begins to pout, sulk, stomp her feet, and make critical remarks about me. If I continue ignoring her, it's not long before she is screaming, crying, yelling at me, and sometimes kicking the furniture or pulling her hair violently. Usually I end up shaking her and putting her in her room. After she calms down, I try to talk with her and let her know I love her. But what can I do to stop these tantrums?

Answer

The chain of events that leads to the behavior tends to support the behavior. To understand how to control tantrums, we must examine the chain of events leading to the behavior. First of all, the daughter asked for something that wasn't appropriate. In many homes where tantrums are a problem, the rules are implied, not specific. Part of the solution to overcoming tantrums is to make sure that the daughter understands clearly just what is off limits so that she is not continually testing the rules of the home.

Furthermore, the cuddling after your child calms down reinforces the tantrums. Rather, stop whatever you are presently doing as a result of the tantrum. Here are some guidelines that may help you.

First, give your daughter verbal permission to throw a tantrum. Call her off to one side at a time when she is least expecting it and tell her that you have decided that it is all right for her to cry and scream when she doesn't get her way. Then, when she throws a tantrum, rather than trying to ignore it tell her it is fine with you and that you will wait for her to finish. Be sure to tell her to throw the best tantrum she knows how to throw. Then stand by and watch without getting personally involved, especially during the heat of the crisis (unless, of course, she is being very destructive). Intervention will only serve to reinforce the tantrum.

Next, catch your child when she is being calm and reward her for it. While she is calm, remind her that she is living by the rule of self-control and compliment her for learning how to take care of problems in a more constructive way. As she begins to cope with situations she does not like in a more positive way, reinforce this with praise, compliments, touches, hugs, smiles, or other forms of contact. (I don't mean money, M&M's, food, toys, or the like. These material rewards may be appropriate for accomplishing specific tasks, like keeping her room clean for a week, but over the long run these material reinforcers have less lasting impact than emotional rewards.)

Recognize positively the times when she is calm after being told no, and encourage her to continue this behavior. The most important thing for defusing tantrums is to refuse to reinforce them: and both ignoring and combating are reinforcing behaviors! So again, give your child permission to throw the tantrum and wait for her to finish. Then, when she has calmed down, talk to her about controlling her behavior. Some parents use a "time-out" chair when a child is losing control of her emotions. If the tantrums persist or continue in school, you may want to seek the advice of a professional therapist who can give you suggestions for dealing with your daughter's frustrations before they blossom into a full-blown tirade.

Ignoring

4

Question

My fourteen-year-old boy needs daily medication, but I have to remind him constantly or he absent-mindedly forgets to take it. I once let him go for a week without nagging him to take the medication, and even though he became tired, lethargic, and ill, he still forgot to take it. I can imagine myself calling him on his wedding night to remind him to take it. But his forgetting the medicine isn't the whole problem. He seems to be in a stupor whenever I speak to him. He ignores anyone who seems the least bit demanding. My oldest daughter thinks he's a "space-case." What can I do to get him to be more responsible and stop ignoring me?

Answer

If your son is a "space-case," he is a very bright and resourceful one. He has induced a lot of people to work very hard to keep him functioning. And you're right—he is learning to be irresponsible. Usually we deal with passive people who sit back and ignore their responsibilities by energizing ourselves, doing much more than our fair share. We may give advice, "do" for them, pave the way, or otherwise try to be helpful, and our attempts usually end up in disappointment. Your son ignores you (probably unconsciously) as a passive way of getting out of doing things and at the same time keeping you over-involved.

The first thing you must do to overcome this problem is to stop doing whatever you're doing now. If you're constantly reminding your son to do things—stop! If you do his chores, answer his questions for him, or become energized whenever someone expects something of him, stop it. Become more passive yourself. (Some theorists call this "selective incompetence.") When you become selectively incompetent, you decide what you are not willing to do for another person because you can just no longer do it. This forces the other person to take care of himself. Remember when you make this decision that your son may try even harder to get you involved, but you must shift the responsibility for his lack of performance back to him. Get him to tell you what *he* will do about his duties and then stand back in the shadows and watch.

If he does what he says he will do, then reward him. If he doesn't, suspend some of his privileges. For example, you may want to withhold financial support or stop providing taxi service when he wants to be taken somewhere. Stop reminding him to take his medication. Define consequences unrelated to the medication: no transportation, telephone, laundry, preparing his meals, and so on. This will certainly get his attention and may stir him to take a more active part in his own life or at least to negotiate about what he *is* willing to do to retain his privileges.

Finally, help him set a goal to become more responsive, such as, "Pay attention when I talk." Then help him achieve his goal. Move closer to him when you talk, or touch him. After you have given an instruction, simply ask him to repeat it to you. These actions will force him to focus attention on what you're saying and help you to feel better understood.

Remember, don't fall into the trap of "doing" for him and answering for him. The reward of ignoring you is clear—he gets you to take care of him! It's natural to assume responsibility for people who are not taking care of themselves as they should; but from a realistic perspective, if we reduce the amount of support that we give passive people they will become energized into acting and making decisions for themselves.

Communication Lines   5

5

Question

I have a quiet fourteen-year-old daughter. I asked her to give me her honest opinion of how I was handling a problem we were having in our home. After some thought, she told me her true feelings. I was terribly hurt and showed it. I could see that my reaction made her upset and defensive. After I gained my composure I apologized, but I can still see that she is reluctant to open up with me now. What can I do to open the channel of communication?

Answer

Your experience is very similar to that of many families I have worked with who have teenagers.

I typically find that families who report a breakdown in communication with their teens never really had a pattern of communication before their children became teens. If you will think back a few years ago, you will

likely see that there was little *two-way* communication
between you and your children. What happens to many
parents is something like this: When our children are
young, we listen to them after they *insist* on our attention
either through negative behavior or by complaining that
we don't listen. Otherwise our attempts at communicating with our children usually follow a "we talk, they tune
out" procedure. Families with poor patterns of communication usually maintain them, and families that have
open channels of communication usually stay that way.

Recently I had an appointment with a family deeply
concerned about the sixteen-year-old son's defiance and
resistance. He was doing poorly in school, had been
caught skipping classes, and had even had a serious
blowup with one of his teachers. I remember clearly the
feeling I had as the eight members of the family sat in my
office. Tension! The family was pressurized to the point
of eruption, and unknowingly all of the members of the
family were doing their best to avoid what each must
have perceived as a potential disaster.

I began the session by asking each member of the
family to give me his or her perception about the problem. Each in his turn pointed at Tom as the culprit; he
was the cause of all the family's ills. And then it was
Tom's turn. Not a word. His head was down, and his
hair flopped over his dark eyes, which were fixed firmly
on his knees. After a few seconds the father turned to me,
saying that no one had been able to get anything but sar-
casm, criticism, or hatred out of the young man for a
very long time.

I said, "Well, someone must get through to him"
—which was precisely the point. No one in the family
was making contact with him. I then said to the father, "I
want you to try to make contact with your son."

He looked at me incredulously, as if to say, "But I've tried, it's hopeless." He asked me to suggest a way to get through. I suggested that he start with "How are you feeling?" So, quite mechanically, he said, "How are you feeling about things?" Not a word came from Tom. He wouldn't even acknowledge that he had heard his father. After about ten uncomfortable seconds, the father turned to me and said, "See, he won't talk."

"Aha," I said, "now we know at least one of the problems: you're giving up trying to communicate before you have even begun. Do you really want to make contact with your son?"

A more sincere and desperate "Yes, I do" came from the father—not directed toward me, but to his son, who incidentally peered up through his hair to see if his father really meant it and then looked away.

I then suggested to the father that he try again, but a little harder. He looked at his son, leaned forward, and said in a very concerned voice, "Tom, please tell me how you are feeling." Again silence. The father looked at me and was about to speak when I silently put my finger to my lips, signaling him to wait for Tom to reply.

The first three minutes of silence were terrible. Every person in the room wanted to speak but was silenced. After ten minutes of silence, the pain in the room was almost unbearable. After fifteen minutes, to everyone's amazement, a tear fell from Tom's eye, and then another until he was quietly but forcefully weeping. At this point, both mother and father were also crying. After twenty-five minutes of silence, I could see Tom's jaw muscles starting to unhinge, and then the silence was broken. Tom raised his head and in a broken voice said the very thing that both parents were afraid to hear and were working so hard to avoid. Through his tears, with no criticism or anger, just honest, deep-down truth, he said, "I don't feel loved."

The blow was crushing to everyone in the room; and yet, as if they had rehearsed their response, Mom and Dad and Tom all stood up and embraced. They caught each other and held on for dear life, and then all the others joined in. You could feel the doors of communication bursting open.

Our remaining sessions were few and constructive. They were sessions where the family members learned to talk to each other. They learned quickly to negotiate and solve problems. Tom responded immediately.

The point of this story is that communication takes sincere effort, probing yet open-ended questions, and listening. Most families never get past the opening question.

To open up communication channels in your home, particularly since your daughter did show positive signs of openness at first, your specific challenge is to convince her that you are sincerely interested in trying to talk with her without overreacting. There are several ways to show that you're interested. You could listen to her music or take up an activity that both of you could be involved in. A great deal can be gained by sharing time with her. Think of ways to spend more time together. These things in and of themselves should open things up between you. When your relationship is better, then:

1. Ask an open-ended question.

2. Listen!

3. Reflect on what you think your daughter has said. Don't jump in to give advice, criticize, preach, teach, lecture, or be too interpretive.

4. Encourage her to expand on what she has said. "Tell me more" and "I'd like to understand that better" are helpful ways for you to draw close to her.

5. Respond to her with phrases like "I think" or "I believe," rather than "You make me feel," etc.

My last suggestion to you is this: Try to see your daughter, her life, her thoughts, and her honest feelings as *hers*, not *yours*. If she disagrees or doesn't like something about you, those feelings belong to her; they're her point of view. Deal with them in that way. They affect you negatively only if you let them.

Fighting and Quarreling 6

6

Question

Our children are constantly fighting with one another. Sometimes they get very physical and other times they just rip each other apart with sharp tongues. As parents, we've tried ignoring the problem, but when they fight we feel we have to intervene. Nothing seems to be working. Do you have any suggestions to help our children get along better?

Answer

To begin with, let's look at some of the reasons why children fight. Many children have the need to feel superior, and fighting is one way to grab the top-dog position. It is very easy for a child to get hooked on fighting whenever he feels that his status is threatened. In addition to this, you parents may be modeling competition in your house. If you, your husband, or both are particularly competitive people, you are setting an example for your children which suggests that there should always be a winner in every controversy and that to take a competitive and superior position in life is desirable.

Perhaps your children are fighting to get their parents' attention. You can determine this by looking at the cycle of interaction that leads up to the fighting. For example, if you notice one of your children setting up the other for a quarrel in order to draw you or your husband into it, then that may be the underlying motive for the quarrel. Your involvement may help to perpetuate this vicious cycle. You can find out if this is the problem by simply stepping out of the fights and watching. If they quarrel less, then what they really want is your involvement.

Another possibility is that your children may have limited emotional outlets. In other words, your children know of few ways to release their energy other than quarreling. If one of your children can get his brother or sister to carry on an emotional battle with him, this often creates a negative bonding which, for some children, is better than no relationship at all. If the climate in your home doesn't allow for some consistent openness and sharing of positive and negative emotions, then your children may be resorting to more volatile means of expression as a release.

A fourth possibility is simply that your children are learning to argue, to defend themselves, and to take care of their own personal needs. For children under ten, this is especially important. At a young age, most children will try to maintain their egocentric orientation in life. It's likely that if any other member of the family challenges your child in these years (three to ten), an argument will ensue, if for no other reason than to defend his own self-oriented point of view.

The best way to help your children learn new ways of handling their arguments is to make a "we talk, we don't fight" rule. Make sure that you remind your children of this rule periodically so that they are aware of the goal you're trying to achieve. Whenever your children begin to argue, remind them of the rule; and if the argument persists, you may want to separate them until they can get their emotions under control and learn more productive ways of handling their conflict. This is the second point I want to make.

You as referee can sit your children down face to face (when they are not emotionally high strung or fighting) and learn how to talk about their problems. In these sessions, teach them how to solve problems, how to compromise and give in. Then talk about ways to resolve conflicts in the future. Set specific goals for this. In my own experience as a parent, I ask my children to talk about what they want their relationship with each other to be like. I ask them if they feel satisfied with the arguing and the fighting that they engage in, and if they would like a better friendship with each other. Usually, when I have done this, my children agree that they want to be friends, but are unsure how to work it out. At these times, as referee, I can step in and make suggestions. By this point in the discussion, my children are more receptive to my advice than when I am confronting them in the heat of an argument.

A third suggestion that I have found helpful in my own home is to teach my children how to "tattle" in a positive way. On special occasions we've given our children the specific assignment to report in a family meeting a good deed that someone else has done. This helps them to turn away from their egocentrism and take note of the positive qualities and characteristics of others, which should diminish the need to quarrel with them.

A fourth important idea is to teach our children how to talk rather than fight. This means that you must model talking and listening that they can see and emulate. After you have set the goal of talking and not fighting, you might spend several evenings during the next month or two actually practicing just talking with each other and learning to listen. This very rudimentary step-by-step approach is a good way to help your children release their feelings of frustration and resolve any misunderstandings that might be going on. It will also help reduce the amount of tension which can lead to arguing. Above all, when you find your children are learning to cooperate with each other, be sure to reward them as often as cooperation occurs. In this way you can help your children learn how to become better citizens at home and to get along better with other people. These skills should translate into positive social values which will help them throughout their lives.

Whining 7

7

Question

One of my children is a whiny, clinging child who follows me around all the time. If I try to discipline her, she whines and complains; but if her father asks her to do something, she responds very well. I need to know why my child whines only with me and what I can do to stop her.

Answer

The tip-off to this one: your daughter is a whiny clinging vine *only* with you! The key to the solution is in your own reaction to your daughter. Look carefully at the sequence of events which triggers her misbehavior, and you'll find that you are very much involved. Your way of solving the problem may *be* the problem.

If for example you try to ignore her wailing until you can't avoid it, she has you trained to give her the attention she wants. If you find yourself telling her to stop whining and she continues until you blow up, she is also getting her pay-off. Neither ignoring the behavior nor attacking it works very well. Watch carefully and you'll see how your involvement in the process may actually reinforce her fretting.

I suggest that you take your daughter to one side when she is behaving well and tell her *two* contradictory things. (Psychologists call this paradoxical injunction.) Tell her, "I want you to learn to control your whining," but "if you need to whine, I want you to."

Obviously, this will confuse your daughter, but don't explain to her what you're doing; just repeat the double message. Then, the next time she begins to whimper, say, "Very good, go ahead; I'll wait for you to finish." Then go about your business. When she stops whining, pay attention to her and compliment her for controlling herself. After two weeks of this, she should have completely stopped whining. Involve yourself directly, set clear goals, and then get her "unhooked."

Remember too that your daughter might be expressing an urgent need through her whining. She may feel a lack of contact with you, particularly if your only real contact with each other is your reaction to her whining. If your daughter whines for more of your time, be sure to give it to her. Find ways of being alone with her. Try to catch her when she isn't wailing and give her some attention. Calm down, expect less, and reward your daughter with praise and time. This will likely stop the whining in a hurry.

Sassiness

8

Question

My nine-year-old son sasses back at me every time I ask him to do something. What can I do to stop him from talking back to me so rudely?

Answer

Before I talk about solutions, let me talk about the possible causes of a sassiness problem. Many children talk back to their parents because of a combative atmosphere in the home. Parents' constant reprimands (logical as they may seem) may cause the child to become frustrated and explosive. In the past I have worked with several families trapped in this negative cycle. When parents demean or criticize their children in an attempt to explain the importance of family rules, the child will rebel—no matter how logical the rules may be. In a sense, such parents are using logic to bop the child on the head. The child's violent reaction is then viewed by the parents as irresponsible "sassing" and they become even more logical or more combative, perpetuating the cycle. Parents who wield logic as a weapon shouldn't be surprised when a child contradicts them or sasses back. In addition parents who lose emotional control of themselves often make excessive demands on their children. This is the classic set-up for sassing. The child is sassing back as a way of combating these unreasonable expectations.

Examine yourself—is your communication with your child a belittling form of logic or emotionally charged harangues to get your children to do things? If so, you've found the source of the problem. Ask yourself what events lead to this sassy behavior: is your own sharp tongue your child's chief model for communication? Is it your style to battle out your differences as parents? Your children may pick up these contentious habits naturally as acceptable ways of solving problems. The simplest way to handle a sassy mouth? Eliminate the child's need to be sassy.

Assuming that you are not the kind of role model I've described, here are a few specific ideas for a relatively effortless solution to sassy behavior. Start with a paradoxical injunction—give your child permission to sass you whenever he needs to. Tell him privately that you are concerned about his back-talk, but that since he must have some need to sass, you're willing to let him go ahead and fulfill that need. Say, "I want you to stop sassing, but if you must sass, go ahead and I'll wait for you to finish." Then disengage yourself and just observe his sassing rather than reacting to it. Since a sassy child wants control or power over people, possibly to avoid uncomfortable interaction, this paradox should take all of the wind out of his sails. Viktor Frankl called this "spitting in one's soup." When you give permission to the child to sass you, he loses the reinforcement for sassing that he once had.

Next, never cooperate with a child who is talking back to you. Set a goal to talk more calmly with each other and solve problems in a more constructive way. Emphasize that you will not discuss anything with a sassing child. Help your children learn that a quick tongue will not get them what they want. If they understand that you won't make any decision in the heat of conflict they will begin to bring their insolent language under control.

Third, remember that fighting with our children or ignoring their sassing usually makes them more powerful. Trying to overpower a child with our own disrespectful talk models the very behavior we are trying to eliminate.

Finally, involve the whole family with rules and goals that stimulate talk rather than fighting, that encourage respect for one another's needs rather than manipulation. A simple rule such as "Talk, Don't Fight" seems to be very useful and helps the child to understand the direction in which the family wants to go. If everyone in the family shares the goals to solve problems calmly (beginning with the parents!), sassiness should cease to be a concern.

Depression 9

9

Question

I have a six-year-old son who is basically a very good child. But when he doesn't get his way, he will often say things like, "I might just jump out the window," or "I might shoot myself and die." He says this with hurt in his voice and tears in his eyes. Lately he has been more and more negative about life and seems suicidal. Can a child this young be depressed and even suicidal?

Answer

At first glance, your child may appear to be unhappy —possibly to the point of depression. A closer look, however, tells me that he is neither depressed nor suicidal, but manipulative. Before I give you specific suggestions as to how to handle this problem, let me tell you about depression in children.

The Mental Health Association of Utah reported in 1979 that as many as twenty children in every hundred may suffer some symptoms of depression—and the numbers are growing. In fact, the rate of depression for one peak period in youth outstrips reported depression in middle-aged persons and is exceeded only among the elderly.

The symptoms of depression in children are sometimes referred to as "masked" symptoms because they typically show up as behaviors that are nearly the *opposite* of symptoms that are typical of adult depression (sleep disturbances, eating habit changes, lethargy, hopelessness, immobility). This "masked depression" in children is sometimes misdiagnosed as hyperactivity, delinquency, school misbehavior, or psychosomatic illness. In other words, children who are truly depressed are seldom morose or despondent; more typically, they become overactive, restless, or uncontrollable in an attempt to ward off the unbearable feelings of despair.

It's hard to imagine a child becoming depressed, but it does happen. True depression in children is usually traceable to a clear cause, usually the abrupt loss of a loved relative or close friend. And its cure usually lies in taking steps to correct or compensate for the child's loss. Many children who are depressed also have one or more parents who are depressed. In fact, some research suggests that children can be born with a susceptibility to the condition. Whereas the depressed parent "slows down," the depressed child does the opposite. Thus if you notice lack of confidence, feelings of worthlessness, helplessness, and unwarranted fears accompanied by hyperactivity, uncontrollability, poor concentration, and persistent physical complaints, and if these occur in relation to a traumatic life event, then your child could be depressed. If removing or changing the traumatic circumstance does not relieve the problem, then *get professional help.*

Now let me respond to the original question. It seems to me that your child has learned a way of getting your sympathy, cooperation, and attention most skillfully. You can be proud of the fact that you have a bright, imaginative, and skillful child; on the other hand, to allow this kind of threatening and manipulating to persist would be a serious mistake.

Any strategy I might suggest for your child must be centered on an understanding of what your child's reason is for going to all this trouble to get his own way. Usually a child tries to manipulate in this way to feel powerful. The need to feel powerful has its roots in his fear of being inferior, or not being important enough to get from you what he needs without this "game." Your job is to take the steam out of the game and at the same time meet his needs for security.

Take the steam out of his game by taking him aside when he is acting "normal" and saying, "I've noticed that when you don't get what you want, you threaten me. I've decided that you may threaten if you need to. I'll practice being calm, and you do what you need to. After you're finished, I will still expect that you do what I ask you to do." (In a nutshell, you are saying: "I want you to learn to obey, but if you need to resist I *want* you to.") Then the next time your child threatens you, say to him, "If you need to threaten, go ahead; I'll wait for you to finish. I still want you to do _____."
Then go about your business and let him try to manipulate. Remember: if you tell him to manipulate and he does it, he is no longer a manipulator; he is now an obedient follower. You might even praise him for following your directions.

Once you have shown him that his manipulative strategy won't work anymore, the next thing to consider in dealing with this problem is your child's very real need to feel secure and loved. One way to start giving him the reassurance he needs is to watch for opportunities to catch your child doing good, and praise him for those acts. Calm down and hug more, give more warm contact when he's least expecting it. Finally, make sure that you have clear rules established in your home and that you are trying to be consistent in their observance.

To summarize: (1) Eliminate his manipulation strength by telling your child to try to manipulate. (2) Help your son understand what you want from him: self-control. Be a model of that responsible behavior yourself. (3) Increase your warmth towards him. (4) Establish and maintain clear, definable rules for him and the family in general.

Stealing 10

Question

My eight-year-old son has a problem with stealing. He takes things from classmates, steals from stores, and has even taken some of my husband's rare coins and given them away. We've tried every type of discipline we can think of. We've spanked him; we've made him take the stolen item back and apologize or make some other repayment; we've grounded him, threatened, pleaded, and even had him stay with an uncle and aunt for the summer. Nothing has worked. He is our youngest son (our oldest son died six years ago). What can we do?

Answer

The best thing you can do for a *serious* stealing problem is get help for the whole family from a professional. A psychologist who has had experience in treating child disorders is likely the best professional to start with.

For less severe stealing problems you must first realize that most children at one time or another steal things.

(You may remember the first time you took something that didn't belong to you. Do you recall your excitement, your guilt, or your sense of power?)

But when your child steals more than once or twice, he may be trying to tell you something.

First, he may be feeling left out—perhaps left out of the family, or dad's life, or a brother's friendship. Secondly, stealing is a sign of low self-worth, which is closely connected with not feeling like you belong. Our self-worth becomes shaky if people don't talk to us regularly with respect and interest, if they don't listen when we try to express our inner feelings, and if they don't expect anything of us. Sometimes we can feel worthless when we never feel we have done anything right, or at least no one seems to recognize our efforts.

A third reason why children sometimes steal is that they are angry or rebellious, and stealing becomes a way of taking their frustrations out on others. If this is the case, the payoff for stealing is not the item that was taken from someone else, but the hurt they think they can inflict. It gives them a sense of power over others.

A fourth reason why children steal is to get attention. This is a tricky form of rebellion, because deep down the child hopes he'll get caught and receive involvement in the form of discipline from his parents. In this case, the stealing pays off in the form in increased *negative* attention from you, his parents.

This is only a partial list of reasons for stealing, but I think it covers the most common circumstances. Now, what can you do about your stealing child?

First, be direct. Establish the rule: We respect other people's property. Let the child know that you are going to help him learn not to steal.

Second, Reduce the rebellious aspect of stealing by telling him to do the thing you want him to stop, but in an acceptable way. That is, tell him that if he must steal, you would like him to steal a special dollar which the two of you can hide so that if he feels the urge to steal he can steal the hidden dollar.

Third, Raise his feelings of acceptance and self-worth. Increase the amount of warm contact you have with your child. This is particularly important for Dad.

Fourth, Make sure your child feels secure and that he belongs. This can be accomplished through clear and specific family rules, and a lot of loving contact. Establish structure in your home.

Fifth, praise your child when he *doesn't* steal. "Catch" him leaving others' property in its place, and when he does, yell whoopee!

Sixth, try not to label his behavior as stealing, and don't label him as a thief. That will only reinforce his unacceptable behavior.

Do all of these things and the stealing will likely stop. If it doesn't, get professional help.

Allergic Reactions

11

Question

What are your thoughts about "allergic reactions" and such ailments as low blood sugar? Do you accept them as genuine illnesses?

Answer

Yes. However, there is considerable uncertainty about the causes of these ailments. Without a doubt, there are numerous biological factors that contribute to allergic reactions and low blood sugar, or hypoglycemia. But there is also evidence that these common physiological problems can be mind-induced.

Psychologists have learned that in many patients, allergies and hypoglycemia are largely problems of emotional sensitivity. That is, the symptoms can be greatly reduced simply by decreasing the patient's preoccupation with the illness. This is true of many diseases. Researchers point out, for example, that people who believe they will catch cold if their feet get wet have a greater likelihood of catching a cold than people who don't think they will necessarily catch cold if their feet get wet.

In short, parents should understand that allergic reactions, low blood sugar, hyperactivity, and other ailments may truly be physiological in nature, but that paying too much attention to these problems can add up to a preoccupation that simply makes them worse. For example, if your child is made to feel emotionally sensitive to the problem, or if he's continually being reminded not to get near a particular item because he will have a reaction to it, chances are better that he will.

Ulcers, allergies, and hypoglycemia have all been shown to be stress-related. If your home environment is particularly stressful—if, for example, you expect perfection from your children, socially and academically—every effort should be made to reduce that stress.

One way to test whether the problem is physiological or stress-related is to dramatically reduce the amount of stress in your home. Pay less attention to the ailment; talk about it as little as possible. If this reduction in sensitivity and stress diminishes the problem, then you can feel reasonably certain that the illness has a psychological component. If, however, the allergic or hypoglycemic reactions seem to be unrelated to any of these environmental or psychological phenomena, you should get medical treatment for the problem.

I generally suggest a thorough medical evaluation anyway. If your child gets a clean bill of health from your family physician but still has the complaints, then get psychological help.

Bed-Wetting

12

Question

Help! I have a six-year-old daughter who has been diagnosed as having a spastic bladder. She wets continually, all day long. Sometimes it's because she has a bladder spasm when she is not near a bathroom. But often it's because she waits until she can't hold it any longer. She's in the first grade and is coming home wet every day. So far, her classmates aren't aware of it because she hides it. I am trying to ignore the problem except that I do ask her to change herself and take care of her bedding. Her response is usually "Okay"—then she puts it off as long as she can and I usually have to ask her repeatedly. She is a very pretty, clothes-conscious, graceful, athletic child, and I adore her. But I am frustrated at what seems to be endless wetting. The smell is terrific. Sometimes she messes. If she goes to the bathroom every hour on the hour, she no longer has the problem; however, she even resists this. I'll tell her to go and she pretends to go and then wets about fifteen minutes later. I am now trying to teach her to tell time so she can go herself. She acts like she wants to learn to be dry and she is worried about whether or not she will wet when she is grown up, but she does seem to have some aversion to going into the bathroom and using it. What can I do?

Answer

The problem of bed-wetting and daytime enuresis is a common one for many children. It's not unusual for children under the age of six to have episodes of bed-wetting at one time or another. However, if your child advances beyond the age of six or never toilet trains at about the appropriate age, there are some basic things you can do to help stop the problem.

1: *Buzzer alarm.* Research has shown that children who have been trained by the use of an electronic alarm will typically stop wetting the bed within fourteen days. These devices employ a moisture-sensitive pad or an electrode that is attached to the child's underwear at bedtime. When the sleeping child begins to urinate, the device detects the moisture and instantly awakens the child with a loud buzz or warbling tone. Alarms of this type are especially effective with overtraining—that is, if the child continues to use the device for two weeks or longer after he has gained control over his wetting.

Some children have difficulty responding to the alarm or learn to outsmart it. If this happens, the following solution should be considered.

2: *Give permission for the wetting.* While it would be a mistake to dwell on a bed-wetting problem to the point of preoccupation, simply ignoring the behavior presents difficulties of its own. For one thing, it's very hard to ignore a behavior that has as much discomfort attached to it as bed-wetting seems to have. As a parent, you would be much better off *permitting* the behavior to occur than ignoring it. In fact, I recommend that you suggest two things in paradoxical fashion to your child: (1) "I would like you to learn to be dry," but (2) "If you need to wet, you have permission to wet for now." If you as a parent can stand back from the behavior so that it becomes something that your child must take responsibility for, this will help reduce the amount of stress surrounding the behavior and the chances are better that it will stop.

3: *Get Father involved.* In many cases where children manifest anxiety through bed-wetting, we can trace the problem directly to fathers who are uninvolved with their children. Some psychologists refer to this kind of father as "checked out." If as a father you are busier than you should be and seem to have little time for in-depth involvement with your family, this may be one of the reasons why your child is wetting. So the third suggestion is to get Father involved. *Spend time* with your child in a warm, supporting, caring, and nurturing role. At the same time, support your wife in other activities which will help take her out of the role of the punitive parent.

4: *"Plant" a suggestion.* Another effective way to help children who have bed-wetting problems is to take advantage of the power of suggestion. Essentially, this means that you sit down to talk with your child in a warm, secure setting just before bedtime and try to visualize the different things that could happen before morning with regard to his bed-wetting.

Use your imagination as you rehearse his options. You might suggest, for example, that when he feels his bladder tighten, he could simply lie in bed and urinate all over himself. However, that wouldn't make him feel very good, and it would be messy, smelly, etc. On the other hand, when he feels his bladder tighten, he could wake himself up and go to the bathroom. That would make him feel proud, and everybody would be happy for him. The idea is to make it obvious which scenario is preferable and let the child *choose* it as the most desirable. In this way the suggestion is planted in his mind; and if you continue this procedure for seven to fourteen nights, the enuresis may well subside.

5: *Don't relate other activities to the problem.* As much as possible, isolate the wetting problem from other aspects of your child's life. I think it's a mistake, for example, to teach your child to tell time so that she can remember to go to the bathroom. My experience suggests that when we make everything relate to the problem behavior, we only help solidify the behavior rather than diminish it. The child should learn to tell time because it's an important skill to have, not because it will tell her when not to wet. Certainly there is a paradox involved in trying to get a child not to wet by reminding him to wet. The more you can isolate her wetting from other ordinary behaviors, the more you will reduce the stress that compounds the problem.

Nonparticipation in Family Activities

13

Question

I have two children who refuse to participate with our family in special activities such as going to church and taking short excursions or vacations. What can I do to get them more involved with us?

Answer

This question could be answered in a variety of ways, depending on the personality of each of your children. If, for example, you have a child who is very clinging and dependent, you might welcome his decision to be alone. If your child isn't a child, but a teenager, then you should perhaps begin to view his nonparticipation as a normal part of a teenager's emancipation process.

But let's assume that you have a child who, for neither of the above reasons, does not want to participate when the whole family is involved. The problem may be that he doesn't like what he experiences when he is with the whole family, or that he wants to gain a sense of identity contrary to the identity of the family. In either case, your child's feelings and behavior deserve some special attention.

First of all, honestly assess the activities you are asking your children to participate in. Check to see if any of the following factors apply to your family-oriented special activities:

(1.) You have a high expectation that your family is to be a *model* family outside of the home. Making a good appearance is more important than enjoying each other.

(2.) The family activities take on such significance that they seem more important than the family members involved.

(3.) You are not listening to your children or involving them in discussions.

(4.) Things must be quiet in the car.

(5.) One or more of your children insist on being the center of attention, which generates rivalries and pulls family members into quarrels with each other.

(6.) Family activities become a battleground for independence.

If one or more of these things is going on during family activities, then perhaps it's small wonder the children don't want to be involved. Obviously, you're going to have to do something to help them see that you're aware of the problem and are determined to eliminate these negative factors.

Now let's turn our attention to some affirmative steps you can take to involve your children more:

(1.) Find out your child's reasons for not wanting to go. Don't preach or lecture. Let him do the talking. The process of thoughtful listening itself will do much to solve the problem.

(2.) Let your child help you develop a plan of action to remove the roadblocks to his participation. You'll be able to tell when he is satisfied that you're trying to help.

(3.) Always be conscious of your child's need to identify himself as an "important family member" and a significant individual: (a) Help your child feel listened to and understood. (b) Get him involved in rewarding tasks that complement his strengths. (c) Get him to talk positively about himself, independent of his brothers and sisters. This is self-validation.

These three processes improve your children's self-concept and help them feel like important members of their family and community.

(4.) Tell your child you want him to go and you expect his participation.

(5.) If the activity is one you won't compromise on and the above steps fail, then set a family rule. For example, "We attend church as a family." If the child refuses, then he loses his privileges and faces the consequences for disobedience.

(6.) If your child refuses to go because he/she is resistant, then *permit* him/her to resist and work at getting at his/her identity.

All of these things together will help you get your child involved. Above all, be pleasantly persuasive and always show patience. Keeping a good, close relationship with your children is more important than any family activity.

Lack of Concern for Wrongdoing 14

Question

What do you do with children who don't seem to feel sorry for wrong behavior? When they have done something wrong and know it, I will ask them if they are sorry or if they feel bad, and they say no. How do we teach our children to have appropriate guilt for wrongdoing?

Answer

First of all, don't shame them into it. Shaming creates excessive guilt. It makes your children believe that they themselves are no good, rather than their behavior.

Several great minds in the field of psychology (Piaget, Kohlberg, and others) have helped us understand how conscience develops. It's a very complex process; but essentially, a sense or feeling of right or wrong comes about by the consistent and firm application of rules, with fair consequences for rule breaking. Or, stated backwards: If we wanted our children *not* to have a conscience or to feel responsible for their actions, we would establish a home where no clear guidelines or rules exist; or we would have rigid, inflexible rules with unfair consequences attached.

Refer back to the opening chapter and review the section on parental agreement and rule setting. Once you have decided what the rules are to be in your home, make sure your children understand them clearly. After that, train your children. Show them what to do, and how to live each rule. Have them practice.

If this is done consistently, they will develop a sense of right and wrong. I emphasize *develop* because a sense about right behavior takes many years to grow. Indeed, children may not develop this capacity until they are well into their teen years or beyond.

So if your children don't seem to feel appropriate sorrow for wrong acts, don't just tell them they should. Rather, set up fair and firm rules with consequences, and train them as to what they should do. From then on, be very patient. Their moral sensibility will come along in due time.

Teenage Pregnancy

15

Question

Our seventeen-year-old daughter recently became pregnant by a seventeen-year-old boy. Her relationship with the father of the baby is shaky and probably won't last. At any rate, they do not intend to marry. Although we have always thought of ourselves as a loving family, our daughter has complained of feeling unloved in the past. Nevertheless, she does want to live at home. We're not sure this is the best alternative for her or us. We feel that our daughter is no longer a child but an adult guest with a child of her own, and that we don't have the same parental role we used to have. Can you give us any suggestions for dealing with this situation?

Answer

First let me say that you should try to persuade your daughter to allow the baby to be adopted. There are many couples who would love to have the baby and would rear him as their own in the love and stability of a family setting. Retaining the baby may seem to your daughter the caring and responsible thing to do, but experience makes it clear that it will introduce difficulties and frustrations to both the growing child's life and her own, and that the child's interests would be much better served by an adoption. If marriage to the child's father is out of the question, I strongly recommend the adoption route.

If nevertheless your daughter will not take this counsel, let me outline four responses to your question and then elaborate. *First*, you are still the head of your home and must maintain a parental posture on many issues important to your family's well-being. *Second*, your daughter is now more of an adult and should be expected to take more responsibility for her life and her child's life. *Third*, the baby will be hers, not yours. She is the parent; you are grandparents. *Fourth*, life will not end for you or your daughter because of this experience.

Let me enlarge on these points. First, you are still the parents in your home. As such, you have a responsibility to make sure that the values and rules of the home stay intact for all who choose to live there. This, of course, includes your daughter. When I speak of values, I am talking about those broad, generally accepted rules of conduct which apply to all, such as:

(1.) We respect others, their persons, their rights of privacy, and their right to have an opinion about their own lives.

(2.) We all help to keep the home orderly, clean, and running as smoothly as possible.

(3.) We all participate in special family activities.

(4.) We talk our emotions out rather than act them out.

In these broad areas of conduct, it is important to

have your daughter agree that if she stays in the home, even though her role in life has changed to some degree, she is still responsible to participate as a member of the group. If she cannot do this, then you may need to help her find a way to be on her own.

You must realize that in a very fundamental way, your daughter has dramatically changed her role in the family and changed the way society will view her. She will be a mother. In spite of her age, she has adult responsibilities and can no longer be viewed as a minor. She should therefore decide for herself what clothes she needs and how to buy them; whether she should get a job or more education; how she is going to handle dating; what she will do about child care and babysitting; etc. In all of these matters you can be there to provide loving support, but it will be your daughter's final responsibility to work out the solutions.

It is unlikely that you can or should control your daughter's dating—whom she sees, how late she is out, or where she goes—as long as she abides by the general rules of conduct you have established for your home and takes care of her child. Taking care of the child does not mean that she leaves the child with you to raise while she works or dates or shops, but that she arranges for these things as any parent would do. If you can and want to tend while your daughter works, you should be compensated.

The key to creating a successful working relationship is to view each other as adults with reciprocal responsibilities. How would you negotiate these same issues with an adult friend? Let that be your guide.

As a mother, your daughter will have the responsibility for the care, feeding, diaper changing, discipline, tending, and raising of her new infant. I have seen too

many examples of homes with your particular circumstances where the grandparents take over the tending,
discipline, and care of the newest member of the family.
This is particularly dangerous, because it fosters role
confusion. Your daughter won't be sure if she is parent or
peer to her child. And as her child grows up, it will not
be sure where its loyalties belong—with grandmother
(pseudo-mother) or mother (pseudo-sibling).

One reason why we slip so easily into the role of
parent with our grandchildren is that we have had so
much practice being parents. We see our children making
some of the mistakes we made as young parents, and we
want to help. Resist the impulse to rush in and solve
problems. Give help *when it is asked for,* and usually in
the form of advice and support. But don't take away
your daughter's responsibilities. Be calm. Simply enjoy
being grandparents. Love your grandchild and your
daughter.

This is a beginning. My fourth and last point is really
the issue I should have started with. In truth, this is not
the end of the world either for you, your daughter, or
your grandchild. An unwed mother in her teens faces
many challenges that others her age may not have to
face. But these challenges, if met with optimism, courage, and support from loved ones, can bring her great
strength.

I could perhaps have written much about *why* this
may have happened. But in reality, the "whys" of unwed
motherhood are complex, and a thorough discussion
might fill volumes. If it has happened, it has happened.
Don't torture yourself or your daughter with lengthy
self-criticism, accusation, or armchair psychoanalysis.
Use this experience as a way to open the door to more

honest talking, more loving and sharing, and especially, more friendship. If you can become a better friend, you may be able to help your daughter navigate the rough waters ahead with more ease. You have not failed as a parent because this has happened. You only fail if you stop loving and trying.

Refusal to Mind

16

Question

What do you do with a child when you nicely tell her to do something about twenty times, and she won't budge until you finally yell at her?

Answer

It's obvious at first glance that asking your child over and over again to obey is not the solution, it's part of the *problem*. Since it doesn't work, stop doing it.

If we look at the dynamics of the interaction between you and your child as you've outlined them in your question, we will find the source of the problem.

As I mentioned above, reminding your child twenty times isn't working—except against you. Stop it. You're reminding instead of yelling because you think you're being kind to your child and keeping your cool. What you're really doing is giving your child a great deal of attention—which is likely the unconscious pay-off she is seeking. (This need should not be ignored. We'll talk about this later as part of our solution to the problem.)

Isn't it curious that our children provoke us until we lose patience with them? As in this example, your daughter could probably tell us what will happen if she ignores your promptings, yet she mindlessly disobeys anyway. Why? The answer can be found when we examine what happens after the yelling. Usually your child runs and performs the behavior as a victim and you watch, feeling guilty. Your guilt probably causes you to give your child praise and affirmation for finally doing the job, but in reality the praise reinforces her disobedience.

Look at the entire chain of events surrounding your problem. Ask yourself: Who does what? To whom? Then what happens? Then what happens? Then what happens? What you are now doing to stop the problem may be the problem. Remember, the solution we use is usually the problem.

Now that you know about the pay-off your child seeks, you can move into a strategy for helping your child be more cooperative:

Step 1. You and your spouse decide that you will work together with vigor and consistency to get your child to be more cooperative.

Step 2. Establish the rule of behavior you want your child to follow, i.e., "We want you to learn to cooperate."

Step 3. Tell the child in the most vivid and straightforward terms what you plan to accomplish.

Step 4. Give your child a double message (paradox) to help reduce resistance; i.e., "We want you to learn to cooperate but if you need to ignore us, we want you to." Whatever your child does, she will be doing what you want.

Step 5. Ask your child to do something. If she ignores you, say, "If you need to ignore me, I want you to." Then shut up.

Step 6. When the child comes to you, repeat the instructions and remind her of the new rule.

Step 7. Reward your child for following through.

Step 8. If your child still doesn't comply, then in a calm way apply consequences which are *tougher* on your child than the consequences of ignoring you.

In any case, spend less time reminding the child of the task. Remind her of the rule instead. Encourage and praise when she does what you ask. Apply consequences for non-compliance.

Lack of a Father's Influence

17

Question

I have a fourteen-year-old daughter who lost her father a couple of years ago. I feel she desperately needs a strong male "arm" around her shoulder and that she should have some form of father's counsel. We have no grandpa, uncle, or brothers nearby. She's hurting inside and I'm finding that a mom just can't fulfill every need. What can I do to help?

Answer

Let me preface my answer with some assumptions about your situation, and then discuss some ways of dealing with the loss of a male figure in your home.

First of all, I assume that your daughter had a good relationship with her father. His loss should therefore cause grief, but if she has not mourned over the loss with some intensity, then she is likely trying to cope by "swallowing" her hurt. She needs to grieve. You can help her do so and to feel understood by talking openly about your own sense of loss, hurt, and grief. I'm not suggesting that you force discussions about her feelings, but that you watch for non-verbal indications that she is holding those feelings in. "Can you tell me what you're feeling?" is a good, direct question for opening up her emotions. This intense sense of loss can occur whether one parent leaves because of divorce or death. The reaction can be just as intense for either cause of the separation.

The second point I want to make is that your daughter may need more intensive help than you alone can provide. Seek out a skilled counselor (clergyman, therapist, school counselor, family physician), preferably a licensed professional in child and family psychology. Certain changes in her behavior will indicate if your daughter's need is great enough to require a therapist. If her school work drops off or if night terror occurs and persists, if depression or anxiety is excessive—these are all signs of the need for professional assistance. If you are not sure if she needs help, ask her. Many of the teens I see have actually asked their parents for help.

I agree about the importance of a strong male model, particularly for girls and boys in their early teens. You should remember, however, that your daughter has had a male role-model for much of her life. During her formative years, she did have a father and this will have a lasting positive effect. Beyond this, your daughter likely has sufficient male role-models in her life—teachers, ecclesiastical leaders, male friends, and neighbors. If you feel that more male contact is necessary, then you should engineer contacts with males. Invite a neighbor, co-worker, or male friend of your own into your world so that your daughter can have contact with them. Your school counselor or psychologist may be engaged to help in fostering contacts.

One caution: Because your daughter has lost her father, there may be some question about her ability to relate properly to males. She may become too energetic about succeeding with a male, perhaps leading to early dating and an early commitment to one person. I recommend that you guide your daughter carefully and monitor her contacts. Don't permit over-involvement before she matures enough to handle a serious commitment. Above all, be open, loving, supportive, and understanding. Enjoy life and help her to do the same.

Baby Talk in Older Children

18

Question

Can you give me any help with my eleven-year-old boy who persistently talks "baby talk"? He is otherwise well adjusted and masculine.

Answer

Your child is entering the age at which most children love to be "center stage." Although he would never admit it, he likely feels as if he's on stage all the time performing for an unseen audience. Most adolescents feel this and act their parts out in an almost ritualistic fashion. Your son's behavior may also be reinforced by any attention he receives for his clowning even if the reinforcement comes in the form of criticism and pleas to stop. Obnoxious behavior flourishes only when someone pays attention to it.

A typical pattern emerges —

(1.) Your child—quite by accident—begins and persists in talking like a baby.

(2.) His siblings and peers reinforce the behavior by getting a big kick out of it.

(3.) You may try ignoring it at first, but finally you try to get him to stop by pleading, threatening, or possibly punishing him.

(4.) He may temporarily stop but begins again in a very short time and the pattern repeats itself.

If this "vicious cycle" is the pattern in your home, then you can help get his behavior under control by changing your own behavior or eliminating the audience. Here are two suggestions that may be useful:

First, look again at the cycle of events sustaining the baby talk. Wherever you are personally involved, remove yourself. Do this by either pretending to ignore the behavior or by paradoxically giving him permission to talk like a baby. Rather than trying to stop it and failing in your attempts, you can now eliminate his unconscious resistance to you by telling him to go ahead and that you'll wait for him to finish. At that point, you go on about your business and pay attention to him only when he's talking as he should.

Second, Remove the audience by encouraging him to talk baby talk only outside or in his room—if the others would like to listen to his gibberish they may join him there. Some may go with him and listen for a minute, but they'll soon get tired of it as well.

Keep in mind also that this is part of a stage and will pass. Patience, confidence, and endurance are the key ingredients to surviving this kind of temporary immaturity. It won't be long before he'll be too embarrassed to use baby talk around anyone. Baby talk, playing with younger children, holding on to a security blanket, and other childish behaviors are not uncommon in children who are struggling to grow up. Give love, room, and patience, and like dirty diapers, this will be outgrown too.

First and Second Child: Same and Different

19

Question

I have heard that a second child will often develop characteristics opposite those of the first child to emphasize his own individuality. Since my first child has many positive traits, will my second child develop more negative characteristics? At times I feel my younger son resents all the good things his brother is doing. How can I encourage my second child to work on his own individual strengths and still emulate his older brother's characteristics?

Answer

In your case, you may be creating a negative "comparison effect" in your children simply by making the comparative observations. Some parents even make such comparisons in front of their children. Try to avoid making comparisons. They are not constructive, they are not motivational, and they are usually contrary to sound management concepts.

You're right—your younger child may resent the accomplishments of his older brother, particularly if they are in areas which you, as a parent, approve of and in which he lacks interest.

Your child may have decided that, since he can't measure up to his brother, he will distinguish himself as "contrary" or opposite to his brother. Let's face it—this is working! You and the family do see them as different. Unfortunately, here we have one child who is OK and one who is not. Both children are victims of their family dynamics.

Your outstanding child may be doing well in acceptable ways to gain your approval; but in a more roundabout way, may not be developing those talents which are uniquely his. On the other hand, your second son falls victim to the belief that he will never measure up and, therefore, does things which confirm this notion.

The cure lies in the philosophical orientation of your family. What is it? Which of these attitudes fits you best—

(1.) We are the best family in the (neighborhood, city, nation, world). When people think of a _____, they think of successful, no-nonsense people who are really doing things in the world.

(2.) Our children have to be better than we were.

(3.) We should expect excellence from each other in physical, emotional, intellectual, and spiritual areas.

(4.) Our children should all be the best—the best students, the best neighbors, the best workers.

(5.) Our family has never measured up with the rest of the world but we're basically OK people.

(6.) We have a family of individuals, each with unique strengths and abilities. Our goal is to help each find his own unique genius.

I believe this last philosophy is the one a healthy family lives by. To arrive at this, consider three courses of action.

First, real effort must be made to teach the concept that everyone is unique—each person has his own talents and weaknesses. No two people are the same. This means that your younger son doesn't have to be just like his brother. He can be different.

Second, when your family develops this attitude, everyone will be less critical, less blaming, less guilt ridden, and each will learn an important lesson in tolerance for the right of all human beings to be different.

Third, this philosophy leaves you less nervous about your child measuring up to some arbitrary "standard" you have created, and permits you to focus on those traits of your child which are commendable. Even if the only thing your child does well is climb walls, recognize and encourage that. Your son will have a greater chance of developing other more positive traits if you praise his wall climbing than you will if you make critical comparisons to his brother.

In a nutshell, the answer is this:

(1.) Develop a philosophy ensuring that everyone in the family is unique.

(2.) Look for, recognize, and encourage respect for each family member's abilities.

(3.) Avoid comparison and competition among family members.

(4.) Love the child in spite of his occasional negative behavior, and convince him of that love.

(5.) Learn to enlarge your expectations of what normal children should be. You'll find that even your less productive son fits into a broader definition of "normal."

Negative Attitudes in Teenagers

20

Question

What can we do for our passive and resistant son who has an "I can't and won't" attitude? He is quiet, but when he does speak he is negative and critical—a dependent child who is resentful at the same time.

I show a lot of love to him and go out of my way to be generous with my time. I think I'm open with him. I keep asking him to do what is right, but he is contemptuous. "Help!"

Answer

Often, in cases like this, parents bring their children to me with a plea to "fix their attitude." I wish I had a magic wand specifically for changing attitudes. I don't, but I do have some ideas that can help you improve your son's frame of mind by focusing on other, more subtle dynamics in your relationship. In other words, I won't tell you how to dictate attitudes, but I will tell you how to modify some of the negative behaviors which account for your son's disposition. The rule is: Change a behavior and change an attitude.

In your question you use three key words which suggest the reasons why your son may be passive yet negative and resentful: "dependent" (Take care of me), "resentful" (Leave me alone [or] I don't appreciate you), and "generous" (I'll take care of you).

Think for a moment about these obvious contradictions in your son's behavior—dependence and resentment at the same time. When children become dependent on us, they do so because they fear what it takes to succeed on their own. In addition, as parents we too often assign ourselves to "do everything we can for our children so they won't have things as hard as we had them." We scurry around trying to be generous with our time, our money, and our love so that our children don't feel insecure. If we overdo it, however, our children will begin to worry about all of this generosity. At an unconscious level they may feel powerless to take care of themselves and may become even more dependent upon your generosity. This dependence usually produces feelings of resentment and resistance.

If we look closely at these three dynamics (dependence, resentment, generosity) we find that one family member is weak (your son), another appears strong (you as the helper), and both are in reality victims of each other's needs—your child's need for help and your need to be generous. When your son accepts your help, he may even resent you for helping when you get so little back from him. In fact, his resentment may stem in part from his perception that you don't need or want anything from him because he's too weak or inferior to give it. This can lead to even more resentment and bitterness.

Now that I've given you a possible psychological explanation for what is happening, let me give you some specific suggestions.

1. You and your husband should agree on the first, most important need your son has in order to become a more functional teenager (see chapter 1).

2. Set a goal with your son to take on more responsibility in the home. In other words, increase your demands on your child. This will make his investment in the family more equal to your own, reducing his resentment and building his confidence.

3. Stop rescuing him. Cut down on your support in food, clothes, allowance, taxi service, laundry, etc., until you feel that he is investing as much as he can in the family.

4. Praise him for being vocal about his needs and for helping out more. Praise yourself for being involved in his life without trying to rule it.

5. Enjoy watching him change his attitude about life.

With this approach, I am suggesting that you not be afraid of your son's negativeness, that you make more demands for his involvement, and that you cut back on your support. This will reduce his dependency on you, lower his level of resentment (although when you get started he will complain even louder—allow yourself about four months of work before you see real change), and will ultimately modify his attitude. His self-control, self-confidence, and happiness will all improve.

Difficulty in Making Friends

21

Question

How can we help our six-year-old child make friends? Nearly every day she comes home complaining that "no one will play with me." We've asked her teacher how she relates with others at school, and she reports the same thing. We've also noticed that she is most content to stay inside when she could be outside playing with neighbor children. What can we do?

Answer

You must teach her how to be a friend! Yes, this is the very best advice that I can give to you. When your daughter complains that no one will play with her, she is expressing a very *real*, personal concern. She may have made some feeble, ineffective, or overbearing attempts at getting others to play with her, but has failed. She may sense a serious inability in herself to develop friendships, while her fear of rejection may cause her to be more withdrawn and even less successful at making friends. It is our job as parents to ensure that she succeeds in learning the skill of developing friendships. Essentially, our goal is to help our children to —

(1.) Be sociable,

(2.) Learn to play with others,

(3.) Be a good friend, and

(4.) Maintain friendships even when conflict occurs.

Helping our children to cultivate these important skills requires effective involvement on our part and confidence in our children's natural ability to learn new skills. Let me make a few recommendations.

First, call your daughter into a private setting for a *private* discussion and tell her that you are going to help her learn how to be a friend. Give a clear, short rule which has *direction.* "You are going to learn to be a friend."

Next, I suggest that you select a girl from her neighborhood, church group, or school who is like your daughter in some way. (You may need the advice of her teacher, a neighbor, or even a church leader.) After you have chosen a potential friend or two, then *force a relationship!* Yes — I am suggesting that you force a relationship between the children. To do this you will have to contrive an opportunity to get them together. (Again, her teacher or others can be very helpful.)

Let's imagine that you have selected a neighbor girl. Explain to the parents of your daughter's "future friend" that you are helping your daughter get better acquainted with children in the neighborhood and that you would like to invite their daughter over for an hour or so one afternoon. You'll be surprised how warmly your call will be received. In fact, it might be helpful to your daughter to see how *you* go about making friends, so invite the whole group over for a get-acquainted evening. You could tell your daughter to "watch how Mom and Dad make friends" or "We want you to see if you can play a little with the neighbor girl tonight."

Finally you should stand back and observe your child's play behavior. If she is making errors in the way she handles her friendships, then these become the focus of your training. You may find for example, that your daughter doesn't share with others. Teach her to share. Set a goal that when her friend comes again that she will practice sharing. Or if your daughter pulls away and doesn't interact with her friend, then she must be taught to take an interest in what others do, to make up games for two instead of one. Role play, rehearse, practice with her at being a friend.

Have your daughter's teacher pair her up with someone at school who may be having some trouble making friends and encourage them to be involved with each other.

Your involvement and her consistent contact with another child will help her gain confidence—you will then be able to fade out of the picture.

Let me summarize my suggestions:

(1.) Set a clear goal with your daughter; don't keep the goal a secret.

(2.) Force a relationship.

(3.) Model how to be a good friend.

(4.) Give your daughter frequent opportunity to practice being a friend. (Don't expect her to develop the skill on her own.)

(5.) Watch in the shadows. Identify any behaviors which don't facilitate friendships and teach your daughter how to be a better friend.

(6.) Praise her for trying and learning.

(7.) Lessen your involvement (fade out of the picture) as your daughter begins to initiate contact on her own.

Question

How can we help our second child develop his own friendships rather than relying on his older brother's friends for companionship?

Answer

I want to answer this question in two ways. Let me give you the easy answer first: if you want some ideas for helping your son formulate his own friendships read the reply to the preceding question.

My second response may seem a little unusual. I feel much less concern for a child who is playing with others, whether his brother's friends or his own, than I feel for one who is unable to make friends at all. It is possible and very likely that your second son plays with his brother's friends because he likes to. He is learning relationship skills with these people just as he would with his own friends.

Remember also that one of the friendships your second son can count on is that of his brother. I see this happen much too seldom in families.

Your son will migrate to friends his own age as he gets older, but for now these older acquaintances are likely helping your son, not hurting him.

Psychosomatic Illness

22

Question

Off and on for the past six months, my son, who is a high achiever, has felt ill and thrown up frequently. He has lost weight, has been to a doctor, and we can find no physical reason for the problem. He entered fourth grade this year and has expressed no real anxiety about school or friendships. How can we help him if his problem isn't truly physical but psychological?

Answer

Your son's difficulty brings a couple of different responses. Before plunging into suggestions about helping your child from a psychological standpoint, I note that you observe no real stressors evident in your son's life. I recommend that you get a second opinion from another physician. These symptoms usually result from physical problems, particularly when no "life events" are occurring which might cause him undue anxiety. If after a second physician's thorough examination you still uncover no causes for the anxiety, then I suggest several psychological helps.

To begin with, I think it would be useful to understand some of the conditions which tend to produce psychosomatic complaints. Such phenomena are generally associated with repression of stress or anxiety, which occurs when we swallow our feelings rather than share them. In other words, when the reservoir of anxieties gets too full, it overflows in a variety of ways. A person uncomfortable with eruptive or explosive outbursts may try even harder to dam up his emotions. When this occurs, unconscious factors tend to take over and the pool of tensions spills over as ulcers, colic, gastric discomfort, infections, listlessness, phobias, or general pain —all symptoms of repressed emotion. This understanding provides the first clue for resolving complaints: Free expression of emotion reduces the likelihood of psychosomatic complaints.

Subtle environmental changes too may lead to psychosomatic illness, changes which have impact on us without our conscious awareness. Disruptions such as a change from a female to a male teacher; new classmates or new neighborhood; the loss of a pet or a family member; even a subtle threat to the family routine—any or all could be cause enough for his complaints. Psychosomatic illness in children is commonly traced to parents who are experiencing difficulty in their own lives and are not coping well with it. If, for example, your marriage suffers from unresolved tensions and friction, your child will likely be affected.

Generally, then, when a child experiences anxiety and lacks the skill to express those feelings, if there are

"stressful life events" (however subtle) which cause uncertainty, or if he is exposed to recurrent conflict in the
home, psychosomatic complaints may result.

Now that we understand some possible causes of
non-physical illness, what can be done about them?

First, express clearly your own feelings to your children. Frequent use of the words "I feel" can teach a child
to examine feelings and talk about them. Set up frequent
opportunities for contact. (Relaxed bedtime talks have
worked well for me and my family.) Take a child with
you on a shopping trip and use this opportunity to communicate. Ask him, "How are things going?" "How do
you feel about . . . ?" "What would you change in your
life if you could?"—or any open-ended question. Then
listen. Sit, don't say anything, and just wait for an
answer. Even if he shrugs and says "I don't know," tell
him you'll wait while he thinks about it but that you're
very interested in knowing. Then wait and listen. This is
how to uncork a brimming reservoir of emotion—to
teach a skill necessary for effective living.

Next, look for stressful elements in his life. Even
minor changes in his environment such as a new bedroom may cause stress. Any change that you as parents
are experiencing may cause your child emotional strain.
If you detect such factors, try to eliminate them. This
should help your child feel less anxiety. If you can't eliminate them, then at least help him to deal with them by
talking about them. The opportunity to discuss what is
bothering us, to feel understood, listened to, and sup-
ported, can remedy almost everyone's anxiety.

Take these steps without showing undue concern,
and you should see the symptoms subside. If the complaints persist, get professional help. A professional

psychologist can often determine the source of the anxiety and teach your son how to communicate and find more productive emotional outlets. If left untreated, psychosomatic disorders can have life-long effects. Don't ignore the problem, but get actively involved in helping your son resolve it.

Discipline for the Preschooler

23

Question

What kind of punishment is appropriate for my pre-schooler? He sometimes becomes uncontrollable and even bites others. When he was younger, I felt that only spanking would stop this behavior, but lately even spanking doesn't help. What can I do to discipline my young children without feeling like a child beater?

Answer

Effective discipline of your child requires an understanding of his functional ability at his age, maturity, and development, to comprehend instructions, to follow rules, and to meet your expectations.

Up to two years of age your child is largely unable to understand even the most fundamental rules of behavior: at this age he lacks the mental capacity to follow rules or even remember them from one setting to the next. Of course, he responds instinctively to conditions which threaten him physically, such as touching a hot stove,

but we call this learning an "automatic reflective response" because it doesn't involve conscious reasoning.
He will avoid touching the stove again, not because he
understands a "rule" given to him, but because he reflects
automatically that touching the stove leads to pain. Observing such a response, we may mistake a reflex reaction
for a more reasonable "rule consciousness."

When you are frustrated that your child doesn't seem
to know or even to learn "what is right," remember that
it is developmentally impossible for your child to be
obedient when he lacks the mental capacity.

At this early age, our children should not be punished
for doing something that we have told them not to do;
rather, they should be directed away from the wrong and
toward activities which are acceptable to you. So re-
direct your children toward something you want them to
do.

The simple fact is that a two-year-old cannot con-
sciously *choose* to behave a particular way because of a
motivation to live by a rule. He doesn't comprehend
rules. Punishment such as spanking is usually not the
best way to get our young children to behave, but if you
do spank, remember that one swat accomplishes the
same result as forty. A spanking may get your child's
attention and create the same sort of reflex response he
would develop to a hot stove, but as parents you don't
want to become a hot stove to your children.

As your child gets older (three to six) he becomes
aware of the existence of rules. The older he is, the more
likely he is to feel a need for order and will even seek to
establish his own rules of right and wrong for his play,
work, and other relationships. Indeed, children must
have rules in order to feel secure and learn about how the
world operates. When you establish a rule and apply

consequences for breaking the rule, your child will begin to see what constitutes right and wrong behavior. This is also the way your child's conscience develops. You can begin to help him develop this sense of right and wrong as he gets older.

Remember, then, that children *grow* into responsible behavior, they are not *born* responsible. Rarely a person as young as thirteen to fifteen years old has developed his rule awareness to the point where he lives consistently by the rules. Be patient with your child's inconsistency. It is true that from infancy your children need order and rules; they don't, however, need to be punished every time they forget. You should expect to be disciplining them continually throughout their formative years.

What can we do then to discipline our young children? (See chapter 1.) Here are a few suggestions:

(1.) Direct and encourage your children to get involved in play or activities that you *do* approve of.

(2.) Remind them of the rule.

(3.) Get them to practice doing what you want them to do. Reward them with hugs, smiles, and a warm interaction when they practice living by the rule.

(4.) Some parents have the illusion that once a rule is learned it should be remembered. Not so. Train your children daily and forgive them frequently when they forget the rules. Remember, they don't disobey because they are devious, but because they haven't developed the capacity to obey.

(5.) For older children map out consequences which are tough enough to deter misbehavior and encourage obedience.

(6.) Stay calm and encourage them. As your children get older, they will becme more obedient. As I suggest in chapter 1: Train—don't punish.

The Single Parent

24

Question

Do you have any advice for single parents? Since my husband's passing, I can't get my children to do anything I ask. I usually have to scream to get their attention and then they still essentially ignore me. When my husband was around, the two of us as a team seemed to wield more influence over our children. Now I feel powerless. Can you suggest how I can get the power back?

Answer

When a person suddenly finds himself a single parent, he should remember that the children also feel a sense of loss. They must now adjust to one parent when they've been used to having two. In fact, your children's misbehavior may be their awkward attempt at helping you solidify your single-parent role. They are likely as anxious to know how far they can go with you, as you are to establish clear family boundaries. In your new role you may be overanxious to be both father and mother. You must remember that in reality you are *not* both. In this double role, you may over-control your children, defining limits and expectations that you would recognize as extreme if your husband were with you. Don't try to fill the gap that your husband left. In all likelihood your style of parenting before the loss of your partner was adequate and should be continued. Overreaction doesn't work and trying to fabricate some compensating "new style" is usually artificial; your children will soon find your weaknesses and shoot holes in even your most reasonable request.

After you take a deep breath and commit to giving your own style of parenting a chance, stop trying to gain more power over your children; this is creating the struggle you are experiencing now, for power plays can produce excessive resistance. Instead, begin to think of ways to get ahead of your children. Be an active influence, not a reactor to crises. Let me summarize this process:

(1). Think carefully about what you want your children and family to be like. Write these expectations down and throw out those that are unrealistic, over-altruistic, or unmanageable.

(2.) Set goals with each of your children individually —in private.

(3.) Apply leverage (consequences) with each child individually—stay out of your children's battles.

(4.) Define your territory—their problems and responsibilities are theirs. They become yours only if you make them yours.

(5.) Call a family council and set *one* goal.

(6.) Discipline in close proximity and with calm.

(7.) Negotiate where possible.

(8.) Keep your cool and remember that every step forward will be followed by steps backwards.

Family management is a continuous process of defining rules and consequences, training, and reminding. Most families never arrive at the ideal. The most important thing you can do is stop the tug of war with your children. Don't try to out-think them, out-yell them, out-smart them, or out-scare them. These ploys never work —they are about as effective as a two-hour lecture. Instead, ponder carefully what you think each child needs to learn in order to be a better contributor in the home. Decide on one goal at a time for each child. For example, your oldest son may need to learn not to "play Daddy" with the younger children; this could be his goal. Set a goal for each child in a similar way.

Next, tell each child individually that you are going to involve yourself less in the conflicts at home and challenge them to do the same. (It is more effective to do this when you are alone together to minimize the rivalry and competition among your children.) At the same time, work out a personal goal for each. Then watch. As he attempts to do what you ask, remember to praise him.

You can engage the positive support of your older children to handle some of the roles vacated by your husband (things like yard work, simple mechanics, odd jobs —even financial planning). Be careful not to give your pre-teens too much adult responsibility. We want to make sure our children don't skip childhood.

If your child is not able to live his new role, then withhold privileges while he practices, so that he'd rather live the rules than face the consequences. My own children feel tortured if they lose their radios or stereos, can't telephone, watch TV, eat Popsicles, or go to a friend's. They know, however, that these privileges can be regained quickly by obeying the rules.

Most important for a single parent, remember that

you really aren't less powerful just because you are alone. You can still set rules and consequences. Just because you are single, you are not necessarily at a disadvantage. Nevertheless, you may be trying too hard to compensate the loss of your partner. This may be causing your over-involvement in your children's conflicts. Try staying out of them—teach them to take care of their conflicts on their own.

Recently, we confined our own children in one bedroom until they came up with a plan for respecting each other's property. They yelled at each other for over an hour, but when they realized that we weren't going to make *their* problem *our* problem, they started to talk. Their plan was simple. They decided to share things and have an open-door policy, but to knock on closed doors before entering. That was a couple of weeks ago and things have been pretty quiet since.

Finally, you'll be much happier as a parent if you can remember that managing your home doesn't end with some magically successful program. Every family has good and bad moments. Parenting is a life process. As long as your children are home, you'll be challenged with the need to manage them.

So take a deep breath and dig in. By the way, take a little time for some personal renewal. Your children don't need you with them every second.

Fear
of Dying

25

Question

How do you help a six-year-old overcome a fear of dying? Recently, when our daughter's grandmother died, she became terrified that either she or someone else she loves would die. What can we do to help her?

Answer

It's important to make a distinction between normal levels of anxiety and a fully developed phobia. In the latter case, your child's fear would be serious enough to hamper her normal daily functioning. If she can't sleep, won't go outside, won't do her schoolwork, begins wetting or in other ways behaves in a much different way than before the death occurred, then she may suffer from a genuine phobia.

However, most children between the ages of four and ten develop some intense fear of something. These fears usually pass without any outside intervention. Typically, our fussing about our children's fears helps to perpetuate them.

If your child's fear is getting in the way of her normal life, then the very best thing to do is get professional help. A family-oriented psychologist is likely the best choice. Ask around and make sure that the professional you choose has dealt with phobias in children and is oriented toward involving each of the members of your family.

If the fear is less crippling, there are some things you can do to improve the situation. First of all, calm down. Don't dwell so much on your child's fear, stop talking about it, and by all means try to resume your normal routine as fast as possible. Second, *do* talk when the child wants to. If your child has serious fears and won't talk about them, she may be reflecting your own fear and concern. Talk openly about your feelings when your child talks about hers (a good general practice for dealing with any emotional upheaval). This will help her feel more secure. Third, encourage your daughter to be hopeful, to remember the good things about her grandmother. Fourth, take steps to increase your daughter's feelings of security. This may include more time with her, more contact, or more routine and discipline. Fifth, teach your child about birth and death. Help her understand the facts about both. Knowledge can reduce fear.

This openness in your home will help your daughter lay to rest the fear, apprehension, and sense of loss resulting from her grandmother's death. If you talk freely and allow her in turn a responsive, listening ear, she will unload about many things. What this process does is give our children a more secure sense of belonging. If they learn to understand themselves they will gain confidence and strength, the very qualities our children must have to cope with life's trials.

Furthermore, open communication allows you to share your grief over the loss of your parent, demonstrating to your child that grieving is all right. When we sense loss, we must also experience a certain amount of grief in order to put the loss behind us. Allow everyone in your family to grieve. Being tough or noble will only delay the outpouring of grief and may actually generate unnatural fear in your child.

Most important—be calm and patient. This fear will pass. If you feel a phobia *is* developing, then get help.

"Checked-Out" Husbands 26

Question

I've heard you and other psychologists talk about the impact of aloof fathers on families. Your description of a father who is "checked out" of the house fits my husband to a tee. I guess that he just doesn't care about me or the kids. The only time he ever seems interested in us is when one of us is completely out of control. If I become overwhelmed he does come to my rescue, but then he becomes too harsh. I just can't win and neither can the children. What can I do?

Answer

Passivity in anyone is hard to deal with. A passive teenager can make generally sane parents pull their hair out. Most people would rather be verbally abused than be given the silent treatment, so I empathize with your dilemma. Let's take a closer look at what might be happening in your home to cause your husband's aloofness.

First of all it is not uncommon for one marriage partner to be more passive than the other. You may have felt in your courtship that your husband's quiet manner was just what you needed—someone to keep you in line, restrained, and calm. From his point of view, that is probably just what he's trying to do in your home now—keep the lid on the family's heat by remaining calm. Of course, from your perspective his calmness doesn't "rub off," but just "rubs" everyone the wrong way.

Sometimes in families we behave in a way that forces a reaction from others, just to see where we stand with them. Teenagers are very good at forcing parents out of their passive shells. It may be that your children are keeping the commotion going in your home just to draw Dad out a little.

Also typically, where one parent is "checked out" the other is very much "checked in." This parent does most of the disciplining, interacting, talking, yelling, encouraging, and crying. In many ways this is exactly what the aloof father wants: a wife who feels responsible for everything. If something goes wrong, it can be her fault. If things go right, he let her do it. As long as he "brings home the bacon" he feels justified in being less involved.

On a more subtle level, a cool father is often just looking for the opportunity to become the knight in shining armor. He simply has to wait for things to fall apart, say "I told you so," and pick up the pieces. Unfortunately this behavior only reinforces the family to try harder for his involvement.

What to do:

(1.) A little planned helplessness on your part wouldn't hurt. In other words, start being short of answers for the children when questions arise. Don't be the first on the scene to correct a problem. Discontinue planning all the family activities and slow down in your reaction time to the problems that come up. This "planned incompetence" will bring your husband into the day-to-day concerns of your family.

(2.) Talk to him. Ask him how he feels about you, your marriage, the kids, and then *listen!* Listen, listen, listen! It may take you several days of listening before you understand—or even to get him to talk at all. Ask "How am I doing?" and then listen. Don't ever answer for him, and make sure he knows that you heard what he said.

(3.) When one parent is divided against another there is usually chaos in the home. You would be better off to adopt his style of management than to be divided. If you let him know that you agree to do things his way and then do them, this should help stir his energy and involvement.

(4.) Talk to him and encourage his involvement. Let him know that you are going to be less involved and that you are giving up some of the responsibility you feel toward the children and home.

(5.) Try to find out what would make him feel loved and appreciated and do more of those things.

(6.) Don't intervene in every child's problem. Give your husband time to be aware and involved himself. And above all, when he does get involved praise him for it even if you don't agree with his method of discipline.

(7.) When he starts talking try to get agreement on where you are going as a family; then let him lead out with the goals that you've set. This will involve him more.

Don't spend so much of your own energy, be a little less responsible, don't beat him to the punch when getting involved—and begin communicating with him. Then he will likely come around.

Shyness 27

Question

What can we do to help our very shy fourteen-year-old daughter? She is a freshman in a large high school and has no friends. She slumps her shoulders and has a negative attitude most of the time. I can't tell whether she is depressed or sad, unhappy or just plain discouraged about being so lonely. We praise and encourage her. But for all of our efforts to get her to be more outgoing, she is still lonely and shy. When she was a small child, her older sister did everything for her, spoke for her, and made friends for her; she had very little need to do much on her own. Her older sister now has new interests and is not as willing to help. What can *we* do?

Answer

What we call shyness is actually a lack of ability to communicate wants, feelings, and desires to other people. This communication block often leads to a poor self-concept and problems building friendships. It's too easy to think of shyness only in terms of poor self-esteem. But it may be helpful to determine specifically which skills your daughter has not developed that she may need to learn to become more outgoing and to take more risks communicating with other people.

Before I give specific hints for dealing with your daughter's shyness, let me caution you. Many parents try to "talk" their children out of their shyness or their poor self-concept. You may frequently find yourself reminding your daughter how pretty or how intelligent or how talented she is—if only she would try harder. But shy people, particularly those struggling with poor self-esteem, believe none of it, and the harder we try to convince them that they are wonderful, the more they talk themselves out of it. When you tell your daughter that she is cute, she may argue the point with you in her mind. When you say to her that she is smart, she may say to herself, "You're just trying to make me feel good; I know I'm dumb." This negative self-talk, common in people who are withdrawn and shy, needs to be understood as you try to help your daughter overcome this condition.

You can't talk someone into a good self-concept. Your child's self-concept will improve as you direct her in certain activities which may not appear on the surface to be related to personality. Let me suggest some activities that help develop a healthy approach to living: (1) talking about and understanding inner feelings, wants, desires, and attitudes; (2) planning and doing some good things on one's own; (3) learning to compliment oneself on positive accomplishments; (4) learning to talk with others; and (5) taking risks socially.

If you want your daughter to learn to be more outgoing and to have a more positive opinion of herself, here are some specific things that you may consider.

First, have more personal talks with her. At first you may find that she doesn't participate with your family except as a listener. It won't hurt to begin making contact with your daughter by talking about your own experiences—without lecturing, giving advice, criticizing, or nagging. Allow your daughter to watch and observe you talking openly with her. Take opportunities to ask her probing questions and then *listen* to her. Most parents become uncomfortable with two or three minutes of silence in response to a question. But children's minds are more intuitive than intellectual, and they need time to mull questions over. When you ask a penetrating question, give your daughter time to think about the answer before you jump in and answer for her or before you go on with another question. Let her be silent until she chooses to respond; and when she does respond, let her know that you've heard what she's said. Don't make judgments about what she is saying. Give her feedback that she understands.

Second, give your daughter responsibility for tasks she can reasonably handle, and then make sure that you recognize and praise her efforts. Teach her to value her own accomplishments when she's done something well and to encourage her in *positive* self-talk: "I see you have done what you said you were going to do with the kitchen. I'll bet that feels good to you. I like this clean kitchen; how do you feel about it?" Then listen to her comments. If she tends to be conditionally complimentary (if she says, "I think it's a good job, but I could have done better"), try to help her to understand that her efforts are useful and worthwhile and that she doesn't have to belittle them.

Third, help your daughter to participate in simple activities she feels comfortable with, first with the family and then with others. (I've discussed this concept in earlier chapters.) This means that you will have to contrive social situations that permit your daughter contact with others who may be similar in personality and circumstance. There may be a high chance of success in involving shy children with each other. You may want to consider inviting a family in your neighborhood over for a barbeque with the purpose in mind of helping your daughter participate in activities, games, and conversations. She may even be given simple assignments that put her in the limelight.

Fourth, set a goal with your daughter to make and keep a friend, then plan activities together which involve the other person. You may need to role play or practice how to begin and maintain conversations, and don't neglect to help her learn to be a good listener and a good questioner. You may have to role-play what to do when others aren't social with her, so that she has an opportunity to practice her response before she is faced with the actual problem.

Fifth, have confidence in your daughter's uniqueness; don't just worry over her shyness. It's far too simplistic to characterize her by one prominent feature of her personality. If we can learn to look beyond the obvious weaknesses of our children, and look to their genius or to the precious gems of potential that they carry with them, we will go a long way in helping them build genuine self-confidence. Never ridicule your daughter when a task is done in a less-than-satisfactory way, and never criticize her in public. That would only serve to convince her of her inadequacy and cause her to withdraw even further.

Sixth, help your daughter to develop a talent she can take pride in and eventually share with others.

Beyond this, remember that the world is made up of all kinds of personalities. A shy person sometimes has advantages that aggressive people don't have; for example, he often evaluates his environment more reflectively than over-stimulated and assertive people can. He also brings calm into an otherwise hectic world. The most important thing I do for withdrawn, shy clients is to show my interest in them and to listen, and my best advice to others on this particular subject is to do the same.

Manipulation 28

Question

I feel that each of my four children manipulates me in one fashion or another. For example, my fourteen-year-old daughter and I are continually in a power struggle. She will ask me to do something and if I refuse, the issue ends in an intellectual argument that she wins. If I have the strength to battle it out with her, I usually finish by threatening her with the loss of a privilege. Then she backs off and sulks, and I feel guilty. My second oldest son, who is eleven, is a very dutiful and conscientious boy, but uses his willingness to help to get special privileges. For example, he will volunteer to clean his room if he can go to the video-game center, even though he has already overextended his privileges. Yet it is hard for me to say no when he has been so willing and cooperative. My third child, who is nine, makes me feel guilty with all his complaints about unfair treatment. It's "Randy's mom bought him a new ten-speed," or "I haven't been feeling well; do I have to do such and such?" My youngest child is an angel, but I have noticed lately that I have to walk on eggs to get her to respond to my wishes. She is always correcting me or trying to figure out my hangups. Her favorite line is, "Why do you always do that?" My question is, are my children manipulating me, and how do I get out of this situation?

Answer

Yes! Obviously! Actually, all parents get manipulated to some degree by their children, and manipulate their children in turn. But when manipulation is the only method used to get results, then families become dysfunctional. Let me discuss just how family members manipulate each other, and then how to avoid the problem.

Needs and Threats. When a parent warns, "I want you to be in by dark, or else," or a child says, "I need to have a birthday party, and I'll just die if I don't," wants and needs are being expressed along with an implied threat of disapproval, disappointment, anger, frustration, or maybe even the end of the relationship. In its most severe form, a family member threatens to run away or violate even the most basic rules of the family. It is very easy for parents to cave in to this form of manipulation and to return such threats to get their children to do their bidding.

Exchange Process. In healthy families, members exchange thoughts and feelings, desires, opinions, and support. But sometimes families experience dysfunctional or unhealthy exchanges when criticism, degradation, or threats of revenge are used to get another person to behave in a certain way. Manipulation occurs when one person tries to use more and more power in these exchange processes to get another to change. I've seen this kind of manipulation at work between a husband and wife who tend to settle their disagreements through criticism. The husband would criticize the wife, and she in turn would criticize him for his lack of effort in certain areas. As I watched, these exchanges would become more bitter and more violent as each traded verbal blows with the other. The intent was to get the other person to change, but "exchange manipulation" was used to whip up enough guilt to force a change.

Intellectualization. Sometimes a member of the family simply out-thinks the others. He uses his gifts of logic to get his way unfairly. He makes statements like, "I'm a responsible person, why can't I stay out a half hour later?" or "If you sleep outside you'll catch cold and miss your soccer game." In these cases, it is very difficult to out-argue the intellectualizer, and his manipulation often works because we cave in to the logic of the argument and end up doing things against our will.

Role and Duty. In almost every family, both parents and children play particular roles. Let's say that your oldest child has learned how to play parent while you're not home. This may even be helpful to you, so you try to manipulate him into other duty-bound roles for your own purposes. Or, if you see your role as a wonderfully generous father or mother, your child may be able to hook you with comments like, "Bobby's mom lets him swim in the river; why can't I?" It is very easy to see the particular roles that our children play, and tempting to capitalize on these roles to get our own gains. Getting stuck in these roles can be very costly, as many times these roles serve to perpetuate the cycle of conflict.

Sympathy. When you or your children take advantage of another's goodness or kindness, you're using sympathy as a manipulator. Sometimes our "do good" intentions produce a "poor me" attitude of irresponsibility in our children. If your children can get you to do things for them by pouting and whining, they're manipulating you through the use of sympathy.

Goodness Manipulation. Manipulation also takes place when your child capitalizes on your basic need to feel acceptable, adequate, capable, level, or just plain good. If you're criticized or questioned or belittled into behaving in ways acceptable to the other person, you're being manipulated.

Plain Threats. If you threaten your child outright with physical harm, estrangement, loss of affection, or punishment to get him to do something, then you're manipulating him unfairly. In each case, the threat makes the relationship more sticky or distant, even though it may motivate the child to do what you want him to do. In the long run, the result will be a poorer relationship, lack of cooperation, and resentment.

Avoiding Manipulation. The way to avoid manipulation is to create an honest and open atmosphere of communication within the family, communication about feelings, emotions, wants, desires, attitudes, opinions, and beliefs. Along with this, parents should sincerely attempt to understand the messages our children send us —both spoken and unspoken—so that we learn to consider what they feel and think before we make decisions that have impact on them. We should exercise influence through example and support rather than threat or force. Remember that you will never be fully aware when you are being manipulated; but even if you are, you will likely be so frustrated that you won't react correctly. To avoid this, determine the styles of manipulation afflicting your home. Give yourself the assignment to practice a variety of responses to manipulation.

Finally, to overcome manipulation, learn to accept the good and bad traits of your family members, and don't be discouraged by the negative. In an atmosphere of honest, open cooperation and understanding, work to mutually satisfy one another's needs. This is particularly difficult when you have very small children, but you can still handle the job if you make legitimate rules in a calm atmosphere, help your children understand their purpose, and take their feelings into account.

Hyperactivity 29

Question

Is my child hyperactive? I have been concerned about this possibility for the past two years, especially after his first-grade teacher called to complain of his excessive behavior in the classroom. He has always been very active since birth and has done only marginally well in school. After his first grade teacher called, we met with her and some other school personnel to discuss our son's problem. She told me things about his behavior which I knew of, but hoped would not be a factor at school. To my disappointment, I found that his excessive activity, his distractedness, his nonresponsiveness, and his emotional problems all seem to be having a negative influence on his school performance. Any unusual activity in the classroom sends him spinning. If he is hyperactive, I want to know it and what to do about it.

Answer

It may be helpful for you to understand the subtle signs that professionals look for when they make a diagnosis of hyperactivity. There are essentially eight signals:

(1.) Erratic and inappropriate behaviors as a result of mild provocation. One of the most easily recognized signs of hyperactivity is excessive behavior which results from even the most mild stimulation within the environment. He sulks because of disappointment, or he may fight with others. He will have unpredictable highs and lows which seem extreme in relation to the situation.

(2.) Heightened motor activity, along with restlessness and agitation, are all associated with hyperactivity. Excessive restlessness is not the only true indicator of hyperactivity. A child can be excessively restless and not be truly hyperactive; however, if he also suffers from other symptoms, then the diagnosis of hyperactivity becomes more accurate.

(3.) Poor organizational ability is another sign. Your child may have a difficult time carrying out tasks in a sequence. If you tell a hyperactive six-year-old to pick up his shoes and socks, take them upstairs, put them in his drawer, and turn off the light, he will likely be confused and not do what you ask.

(4.) Distraction to a more than ordinary degree signals true hyperactivity. Such children are usually thrown off tasks by stimuli which would not distract a normal individual. A car driving past a classroom would not usually divert the bulk of the students, but it may keep a hyperactive child off task for several minutes. Even a classmate shifting in his chair could draw him off and keep him from performing up to standard.

(5.) Faulty perceptions often complicate specific learning problems: reversing letters, the incapacity to represent clear shapes on paper or to read accurately because of an inability to organize the letters presented on the page.

(6.) In addition to having faulty perceptions, many hyperactive children are physically awkward, usually resulting from immature development. This shows up in lack of coordination of gross-motor skills (kicking, skipping, jumping) as well as fine-motor skills like tracing and writing.

(7.) Short attention span is another characteristic of hyperactivity. A good rule of thumb for analyzing whether or not children have the ability to attend to task is to see how long they can stay with it. Usually a child can attend half a minute for each year of age. In other words, a seven-year-old child should be able to stay on task for 3½ minutes without being distracted. Hyperactive children tend to have much more difficulty concentrating.

All of these factors tend to identify the hyperactive child. Typically, the hyperactive child is not just busy—he also behaves inappropriately, and parents have a very difficult time controlling him because of his emotional conflict.

If your child exhibits three or more of these characteristics, there is a good possibility that he is hyperactive. However, before you make that assumption, I strongly recommend that you obtain a thorough professional diagnosis for hyperactivity and learning disabilities. This analysis should include such tests as the WISC-R (Wechsler Intelligence Scale for Children—Revised). While the test gives an overall IQ for the child, its real use is to determine in which specific areas the child may need help. McCarthy's Scales of Children's Abilities is another excellent test for assessing the development of specific learning processes. It correlates highly to the Wechsler scales as far as general achievement potential and intellectual ability, but it also measures the extent to which the child is developing his learning faculties. The Woodcock-Johnson test is good for determining the reading, math, and social awareness of a child, and can be used as an important diagnostic tool for calculating deficiencies in these skills. The Key Math provides specific information about a child's success in math-related areas and can also be used to pinpoint learning disabilities. The Bender-Gestalt Test and Draw-a-Person Test are typically given to help the professional understand the emotional and developmental abilities of the child.

When these tests are administered by a legitimate professional, they can be useful guides in understanding how to treat your child. When you find a professional who will conduct thorough tests, make sure that he is also willing to go to school with you to map out a success program for your child. He should be able to help you understand how to handle hyperactive episodes that come along and give you special hints for controlling your own responses so that you don't perpetuate the phenomenon within your home. I hesitate to give special hints for handling hyperactive children, because this problem is usually too complex to treat with simple suggestions. I do strongly recommend, if you suspect that your child is hyperactive, that you get a thorough diagnosis and examination and professional help for your family.

Nervousness, Hair Pulling, Tics, and Mannerisms

30

Question

My eight-year-old daughter has a serious habit of pulling out her hair. She started this behavior about two years ago when she began twisting her hair and sucking on the ends. Now she twists it until it breaks off or falls out. I have seen her pull out large clumps of hair and then look startled as she stares at it, astonished at her own behavior. She seems tense and preoccupied most of the time. When she is having problems or when we discipline her, we notice that this behavior increases. We have tried to make her aware of what she is doing, but nothing seems to work.

Answer

You have every right to be concerned about this behavior, but you should not feel defeated. Though you may not recognize the things in her life she has to worry about, she is internalizing some problems, and these stresses are expressed through this redundant mannerism. After a while this becomes habit, and that makes nervous symptoms hard to treat. The longer your daughter keeps up this habit, the more difficult it will be for her to overcome it, though overcome it she will.

My first suggestion to you is to take your daughter to a child and family psychologist. Typically, these behaviors are too complex for the untrained to deal with. A psychologist skilled in treating stress-related disorders can help your daughter find the source of her stress and teach her how to relieve her tension other than by pulling her hair out. Your therapist may want to involve the whole family in the treatment of this problem because it is much easier for him to teach parents to give ongoing help than to work it through one-on-one. Typically, when a psychologist works with a person individually, the treatment time is two or three times longer than it has to be if the person can be treated within the context of the family.

Next, consider the number of times each day you remind your daughter to stop pulling her hair out. Every time you remind her, you reinforce the habit by calling attention to it; you increase her stress over her lack of control and create resentment which may cause her to resist *any* suggestions you might give. She may unconsciously choose to pull at her hair even more. While your therapist is working with her, let your daughter engage in this behavior as often as she needs to as she learns alternative ways of handling her stress. You will no longer feel the need to remind her to stop.

Then, when opportunity arises, talk to your child. Help her feel secure and listened to. If you can get her to open up her feelings to you, this will also serve to release tension. You may be able to find the source of the stress and help your daughter understand it in a different way.

Above all, because this kind of behavior seems to be too complex for families to deal with on their own, I strongly encourage you to get professional help. This should provide you the tools to handle this problem, and you will find more success in helping your daughter with related anxieties.

Thumb Sucking: The "Linus" Syndrome

31

Question

My five-year-old son, David, has developed the habit of curling up in front of the TV and sucking his thumb. He is doing it more often now and it infuriates the rest of the family. His brothers call him "sissy" and even his sister seems annoyed. We have lately considered binding his arms and hands to stop the problem. Can you help us?

Answer

Thumb sucking is common among children under the age of six. It is generally viewed by helping professionals as the "security blanket" method of reducing anxiety. You may wonder what type of anxiety a child of five has to deal with. My experience in working with children shows that they experience the same stress that adults undergo over responsibilities, relationships, duties and obligations. Snuggling up to a blanket or sucking a thumb seems to be a mild release for anxiety—certainly less destructive than other behaviors discussed in this book. I remember a mother who in a half-critical way asked her child if his thumb "tasted good." She did this every time he put it in his mouth. I was amused to hear the child respond that it really didn't taste good—but that it wasn't fattening—and then showing no signs of wanting to give it up. The only negative consequences are the possibilities of developing crooked teeth or embarrassing you in public; other than these, your child will not suffer from this simple tension-reducing mechanism. If you ignore it, your child will typically grow out of the problem by about age six. If it persists for very long past six, or if you notice any changes in the structure of the mouth or teeth, then see a physician, dentist, or therapist, who works with this type of stress reaction in children.

One thing you can do to help your child overcome tension is to increase the affection and understanding you give him. This will reduce his need for a "security blanket." Since your child is old enough to understand the things that you talk about, you might discuss how far you will allow this behavior to go. For example, you may not want him to suck his thumb in public or around a friend, and you may want to establish specific limits on his thumb sucking. He may be permitted to suck his thumb before going to bed. You should always keep in mind and make explicit to your child that you are going to help him learn how to control the urge to suck his thumb until he stops. In your question you discussed the possibility of putting a binder or hindrance on the thumb. This may stop the sucking, but it won't solve problems related to tension. Binding the thumb will only reroute the tension, which may then surface in other ways, such as a nervous stomach or even tics. The best thing is to be patient with your child, ignore the behavior, and try to avoid reminding him over and over again that he is doing something wrong. Every time you remind your child that he is sucking his thumb, this will serve to reinforce the habit and increase the chances that it will persist.

Teasing and Bullying 32

Question

How can I get my older son to stop picking on his younger sister? Whenever she is around, he makes fun of her, criticizing or being just plain mean. As parents, we get infuriated with him and seem always to be on his back about it, but we are afraid if we ignore it he could really do some damage to his sister from both an emotional and physical standpoint. Is there anything we can do, anything we have overlooked, in trying to stop his bullying behavior?

Answer

The first thing we must do as parents in trying to help our children work out conflict is to look at the interaction which takes place between our children in a more objective manner. As we do this, we will find that what seems a clear-cut bullying problem turns out to be more complex than we thought. You may find, for example, that your younger daughter subtly encourages the older son to bully her. She may send non-verbal messages to him such as a dare, or put-down stare, or some other covert signal that sends him into a frenzy. If you don't detect these particular behaviors in your younger child, you may ask her if she knows how to make her older brother angry. Many times we find that children know specifically how to get a bully to bully them. Watch what happens before and after the bullying. For example, you may be biting your tongue as long as you can while the bullying is going on, but as soon as you reach your threshold of tolerance, you jump into the middle of it. Your behavior may be reinforcing the problem; you may be giving your son negative attention and helping your daughter feel rescued without being aware of it.

Second, you might ask yourself about the purpose behind the bullying. Are your daughter and son trying to force you to be more involved with them even though on a negative level? There may be other factors, but your present method of solution may actually be the source of the problem. If you are trying to ignore it or intervening every time it occurs, you may be giving negative attention that really isn't warranted. I've always felt that a basic rule of thumb for child management is to let children work out their relationships among themselves; to teach them how to do that rather than trying to manage their relationships for them. Here is my specific advice to you about overcoming teasing and bullying.

1. Begin by changing your involvement in the interactional pattern. If you are reinforcing the problem either by trying to ignore it until you can no longer tolerate it, or by intervening constantly, you may be just perpetuating the bullying. If you're involved in the conflict, get

out. Permit your children to work through their conflict without your intervention. Make this explicit by telling them that their problems are their own, and you're there if they want your help, but for the most part you're going to let them work things out without you.

2. Second, help both children understand why the bullying takes place. Begin by helping your daughter recognize her sometimes unconscious behavior that elicits the bullying response. You might do this by giving her an assignment to *make* her brother tease her. This will force her to see what she is doing to get her brother ignited into bullying her. In the same light, encourage the brother to tease the daughter and make her cry as often as he feels the need to and that you will permit it (this is a paradoxical injunction), but in the same breath tell him that you want them to learn to get along better. He is now getting a paradoxical message: "Get along," but "Fight if you need to." Children typically respond positively when faced with this sort of dilemma, so it is likely that he will become more conscious of his negative behavior and actually resist the temptation to bully his sister. If he bothers her anyway, you can give him a message that you know he is following your instructions and that as long as he needs to, he has your permission to bully; but again, tell him you would rather he get control of this urge and cooperate with his sister.

3. Third, determine your son's and daughter's basic emotional needs. Their unfulfilled needs are the reasons behind the quarreling. Find ways to satisfy their needs when they are being good. Your daughter may need to appear in a good light in your eyes. Find times when she is not being teased to support her and reinforce her. Your son may also want to feel your approval and attention

even though he is going after it in a very negative way. Find times when he is not bullying to share with him, to have warm moments, and to have special contact.

4. Encourage your children to work on their relationship with you as the referee. You may want to refer to my section on fighting and quarreling, where I indicated that you should have your children sit down face to face and talk about what they want their relationship to be like. They will be tempted to talk only about the problem and try to blame each other for things that are going wrong. You may be tempted to pick apart their perceptions of what is happening. Move beyond that. What needs to happen down the road for them to learn to get along? Ask them if they like their relationship the way it is now, or if they would like to be better friends in the future. If they agree to be better friends, then discuss how they can show friendship rather than widening the distance between each other.

In summary, remember to make this problem their problem—with you as guide for finding solutions. Don't always try to stop them or rescue them from each other. Rather, make sure that they are aware that you are going to allow them to work through their conflict; after the dust has settled, sit down with both of them and help them resolve the issues between them. In this way you are helping them to discover how to manage future conflicts, which will in turn help them in their marriages and other relationships as they mature towards adulthood.

Teenage Rebelliousness

33

Question

How do I deal with my fourteen-year-old daughter's rebelliousness? She seems to want to do the opposite of anything I ask her to do. I believe in individuality, but she seems so selfish and uninterested in my needs. Is there anything I can do to help her become more responsive to me?

Answer

The discussion here will be lengthier than the others in this book, because many factors are involved in teenage rebelliousness and the ways to minimize or remove it.

As the connecting cable released, the glider pilot realized that he was on his own for the first time. Navigation had been easy when there was a backup, but now the flight was all up to him. At first, he felt a deep fright. He overcompensated, banked, and veered. He felt for an instant that he had forgotten how or what to do. And then gradually his courage came back, and he practiced his moves to bring the craft back under control. Every act was mechanical at first, but then, relaxed, he maneuvered with near precision. After ten minutes, he felt like a pro, and with some daring, tried stunts he had never done before. As the updrafts subsided and the landing strip drew near, he was momentarily tense again, but then the wheels touched down and his face broke into a spontaneous smile. He had made it, and he had done it all alone. He unbuckled himself and thought, "I'm a little bit better, a little bit braver, and a little bit stronger than just a few minutes ago. Sometimes it's harder but better alone."

Teenage years are like a very long solo flight.

When your children arrive at ages eleven to thirteen, they begin to undergo marked physical, mental, and social changes—their journey into puberty, a process which lasts about ten years. Puberty is a confusing time for parents and children alike. During this transition period, your child may show some of the characteristics of younger children, like inconsistency or tantrums; yet sometimes they will try to copy adult behavior.

At this time in his life, your child rejects his childish behavior, enters a strong peer group, begins organizing life activities, develops adult physical characteristics, and establishes a male or female identity. It is the time for building relationships with the opposite sex, achieving emotional independence from you as parents, choosing and preparing for a vocation, and becoming socially responsible in both attitude and behavior.

As your children enter adolescence, they begin to feel, for the first time, the real exhilaration of independence, although it often creates a degree of insecurity. Occasionally, as your teenager begins to flirt with his

newfound independence he will overcompensate by trying too much, too soon, too often. This may lead you as
parents to do the same. You may overcompensate by trying to impose tight controls or revert to the discipline
strategies you used when he was a young child. You are
aware that these strategies will not work very well, but
you may not know of any other way; and sometimes we
try to treat our teenagers as though they were still children because we are afraid of their new independence.
We forget that we were trying to be good parents when
our children were younger so that they could be independent as teenagers. We want our children to learn to fend
for themselves; and yet, when they enter adolescence, we
become uneasy with their individual choices. We view
these acts of independence as a loss of control, and in
reaction we may panic, retreat, or overcompensate by
imposing unreasonable restraints. These overreactions
can actually reinforce the very behavior that we fear
most; and instead of correcting the problems, our unreasonable attempts at control may increase them. Someone
once said that children are like sunflowers. If they are
allowed to grow and develop with their faces to the sun,
they will thrive. But if they are tended too closely, cut
down, or shaded too much, they will wither and die, or
at least fail to grow up to their full potential. Although
this may be oversimplified, it is a useful illustration. Our
teens need room for growth. We must give them that
room.

There are some striking differences between teens and
children. First of all, the adolescent thinks very differently about rules than do younger children. When a child is
ten or younger, he tends to view rules as a necessary part
of his life. Without rules, he feels insecure and threatened
and may run out of control. However, when children

enter puberty, they no longer view rules as fixed in cement, unbreakable and unchangeable. Rather, they see them as guidelines for living in a society that came about through common consent. This means that teenagers, unlike younger children, will insist that they have a right to an equal vote or an equal say in what happens to them. They usually go along with rules they have agreed on or consented to.

When you tell your teenagers to do something and they ask why, what they want is information. If you respond to "why" with "because I told you so," you are treating teenagers like young children, and you will likely get a hostile, belligerent, or resistant reaction. A teenager's psychological and emotional makeup is well advanced beyond the "because-I-told-you-so" stage of younger children. When you propose a rule, they tend to cast a psychological vote as to whether or not they will follow it. In this sense they are just like you. They resent being imposed upon without an opportunity to voice an opinion. Your flexibility and interest in their opinions will stave off the typical responses to imposed control: resistance and rebellion.

You may feel like another mother who said, "Everything I tell her to do, she wants to do the opposite." When I asked, "What do you do when she resists?" she replied, "I get her father to tell her what to do." It was easy to see that this approach led to more resistance, which in turn pushed the mother and father to try even harder to control their child. The harder they tried, the more their teenager resisted. If your attempts to control create resistance, and resistance leads to even worse behavior, you must back off and do something different. Negotiation is one alternative to control.

A second important point about teenagers is their strong need to feel that those things which are required of them are legitimate. In other words, when you want your teen to behave in a particular way, it must be for a good reason which is made clear to him. You should anticipate the questions that might come up when you ask your teenager to do something and develop a good rationale for the request. Unexplained demands should be avoided because your teenager won't feel that he has an equal vote in what happens. With our younger children, we may have gotten by with being arbitrary, rigid, or less democratic; but with our teenagers, this approach simply won't work. Sometimes we even have to back down on our position in order to show that we are willing to negotiate. Negotiation leads to understanding and agreement.

Some of us think we are understood when our teenager agrees to go along with us, but there is a difference between agreement and understanding. Our goal should be first to understand each other, and then to agree on the rule. We must avoid force or manipulation to get our teenagers to agree. Submission is typically a form of quiet rebellion, and a teenager can learn to rebel within the clutches of his parents just as dramatically as outside.

Negotiation, on the other hand, is a way to show respect for the needs and concerns of our teenagers. We show our respect by listening, and when we listen, our teens will tell us what they need. However, if we view our teens' wants as impositions, they will try to find understanding elsewhere.

Moral reasoning. Some experts state that children pass through several levels of moral reasoning as they grow toward adulthood. At the lowest level of morality, children are motivated to avoid punishment: "If you open the fridge again, I will spank you." Threats like this cause our children to do what we want, but their reason for doing so is based on the lowest level of morality. This is like going to church simply to avoid God's wrath.

A child functions on the second level when he does something with the motive of personal gain: "If you do the dishes, you'll be paid fifty cents." This again represents low morality. If your child constantly does things only to get a reward, he is not developing moral awareness. At this level the child is generally insensitive to others' needs and practices real selfishness.

As your child grows and matures he may be motivated to maintain popularity. This is the third stage of moral development. At this level you might hear yourself say to your child, "If you do the dishes, Mother will think you are a good girl." This teaches self-centeredness. If your child is motivated by popularity, he still has little sense of social responsibility.

At the fourth level of moral motivation your children learn to obey rules and regulations for their own sake: "The rule in our house is that everyone has a turn doing dishes." As they begin to see the rule as valuable to themselves and others, and want to obey because it is good to obey, they demonstrate social awareness and responsibility. This is an improvement, but still lacks real morality because the motivation comes not from doing what is right because it is right, but from a desire to obey.

A child arrives at the fifth level of moral reasoning when he observes the rules because he has promised to: "I will do the dishes because I said I would." This higher motivation shows an internal moral process that is genuine: "I see that my word is important to keep; and therefore I am willing to do it—not to get gain or someone's approval, or to avoid punishment, but because I said I would do it."

We can get our young people to live at this level of responsible behavior by asking them to tell us what they will do and then to commit themselves to it. "I will be home at 11:30" is much better than a parent saying, "Be home at 11:20." At the highest level of morality your children do things because of an inner necessity: "I will do the dishes because I want to be responsible to my family by doing my share of the work." Only then does he show a true sense of personal responsibility.

You can learn to lift your children from lower levels of motivation to higher ones. First, assess how you try to motivate your children now. Do you threaten, reward, praise, or ask for a promise? Your own morality will influence your children's. One of the most common complaints I hear about teenagers is how irresponsible they seem to be; yet many parents try to motivate their teenagers into obedience by threatening them, by bribing them, by withholding acceptance, and by forcing them to obey rules. These lower-level motivational tactics will only encourage your teenager to behave irresponsibly. It is much more appropriate to give your teenager the opportunity to explain what he is willing to do and then hold him responsible for it. Agreement, commitment, follow-through, and reward will bring success in raising teens through high moral development.

Equal vote, equal say: family negotiation. Independent judgment and commitment should be encouraged in your teenagers because these traits foster moral development and responsible behavior. The following tips may be useful in helping them develop positive independent judgment.

Find a time to sit down together to identify specifically what you and your teenager feel he would be able to do about—

(1.) Responsibilities around the house (for example, taking out the garbage, making his bed, and cleaning his room),

(2.) Money management,

(3.) Personal grooming,

(4.) Part-time job,

(5.) Decision making,

(6.) Communication,

(7.) Self-discipline,

(8.) Schoolwork.

It is important that this not be a "we talk, you listen" session. Let your child take an active part in these decisions. One family I worked with called a family council, with this agenda:

1. Father to report on finances.

2. Suggestions on handling the food budget. Each child to make a menu for one month, including preparing snacks and well-balanced meals and shopping for bargains.

3. Reading of each child's personal record of monthly expenditures, including discussion of good and bad feelings about how things went.

4. Plans for keeping utility bills reduced, including turning off the lights when leaving the room and cutting down on the use of hot water. How should we use the money we save by our efforts? Vacation? Savings?

Plan a family council with an agenda similar to this for discussing some area of concern in your family. This exercise will also help with my next tip, which is to increase the amount of dialogue. When you allow your teenager to participate in family decisions that everyone can agree on, this will bring your family together and increase the chance of success. If our teenagers do not feel a part of family negotiations, they are unlikely to cooperate. Help them to feel that their opinion counts and will be considered, and their resistance will subside.

Increase dialogue. To achieve responsible independence and acceptance of family goals, you must keep open the lines of communication with your teenager. To ensure this, you must not be so much a judge of his behavior as an interpreter, who tries to achieve clarity in what is discussed. It has been said that children are good observers but poor interpreters; your teenager may see what goes on—Mom and Dad disagree, have words— and he may conclude that they hate each other and him. You can help him interpret these experiences correctly by explaining what is happening.

During these years your teenager will feel that his new set of emotions is unique to him, that he is different from everyone else, even his peers, and that there must be something wrong with him if no one else is going through what he feels. Long talks about feelings will reduce this uneasiness.

The manner in which we speak to each other is of great importance. It is interesting that we are sometimes more polite or courteous to strangers than we are to our children. We should foster a positive (non-critical), encouraging dialogue oriented toward our best hopes for their success. When you communicate, remember to give your support and talk about your youngster's ability to succeed rather than his failures.

In her book *Parents and Teenagers*, Evelyn Duvall observes that young people don't find it particularly easy to put their feelings into words. They hardly know themselves what they feel. Try asking your upset teenager how he feels, and he will probably say, "I don't know."

This sounds like defiance, but it is really an expression of his emotional confusion. While one teen may express his confusion, another may act out his frustration in rebellious and deviant acts against people or property. Like many of us, teenagers are groping for a new way of life that will satisfy their longings and reduce their confusion. A parent who effectively communicates during these confused times can be like a lighthouse in the fog. Continually assure him that he can talk out rather than act out his feelings, no matter what those feelings happen to be; this is really the most productive way of living. We want our children to achieve some control over impulses, rather than to act out all their feelings as they did when they were children. The achievement of such control is the hallmark of adult behavior. We must model that type of control.

Talk more about what is to be accomplished. The more your adolescent feels his maturity is underrated, the more rebellious he will be, and the more awkward will be his attempts to prove how grown up he is. He needs to be encouraged when his experience has let him down, not ridiculed or restrained. Your adolescent will achieve independence only by trying it out. (See J. Rosewell Gallagher, M.D., *Understanding Your Son's Adolescence,* p. 161.) For example, when you want your teen to keep his room cleaner, make sure he knows that he has accepted full and final responsibility; that it is his job, and his alone, to do; and that he understand what is to be done and how. Make sure you show him how to do it and then let him practice. When he accomplishes all or even part of the task, comment on his positive efforts. This should help your teenager feel more a part of the family.

Give full and final responsibility for tasks. I met one

teenage boy who took lightly his responsibility to take out the garbage each day. Although he had agreed to do it, somehow it never got done. His mother, realizing that nagging only provoked him and made her miserable, told the boy, "You have the right to refuse to take out the garbage. I have the right to refuse to cook in a dirty kitchen with garbage piled up." For three days the mother did not cook, and finally the boy took his responsibility more seriously. If your son has accepted the job to water the lawn, make sure he knows how to do it; provide the proper tools; then let him do it. Sometimes we relinquish responsibility by reminding our children of what they are supposed to do before they have an opportunity to try on their own; or if the task is not done to our satisfaction, we go in behind them and do it our way. This teaches irresponsibility. Be careful not to make the rules for doing a particular job too lengthy and complicated. Stephen Covey, noted author and lecturer, gives his children this rule for lawn care. "Green and clean." Enough said.

Give greater attention to desired behavior. Compliment your teenager when the job has been done: "I like the way the lawn looks, son." Say nothing when it is not done well. Compliment him in front of your friends and relatives, and also his peer group. You may reply, "That sounds easy, but how can I keep my sanity when I like to see things done right and they are not being done right?" I answer that you must decide what your main objective is and then stick to it, regardless of the personal sacrifice you may have to make or what justification there may be at the time for departing from it.

Michael McCarthy told this story at a 1978 health-care convention in Salt Lake City. While waiting in line for tickets at a very busy airport terminal, the prospec-

tive passengers were playing a "kick and shuffle" game.
(This is where you stand in line, kick your bag forward,
and then shuffle up to it.) The lines were long and crowd-
ed, and airline employees worked furiously to please
everyone. One man pushed his way to the front, bump-
ing shoulders with those in the way, and slamming his
hand down on the desk, shouted, "I have to be in Los
Angeles at 8:30!" The agent politely replied, "Okay, sir,
you will be," and proceeded to help the passenger in
front of him. The man stood silent for a moment, growing more angry and frustrated. Finally, he slapped the
counter again and repeated his command. The agent
courteously remarked, "I'll be with you in a moment,
sir," and went on helping those in line. Infuriated, the
man threw his briefcase on the desk and screamed, "Do
you know who I am?" The teller then turned to his fellow
worker and sighed, "Gee, now we have a guy who
doesn't even know who he is." Needless to say, this drew
cheers from the tired crowd, but what do you think the
irate passenger did? He went to another airline, boarded
another plane, and was in Los Angeles at 8:30.

Now, let's go back and see what happened. The
employee was certainly justified in the comments he
made. He might have been justified in saying more. It
was a real treat for the tired crowd, but what is the main
objective of an airline ticket agent? To get the passengers
on the right plane, on time, and to keep them happy. Although his actions may have been justified, they were not
in line with his main objective and so he really lost.

I would suggest that as parents, you sit down with
your teenagers to decide what you hope to accomplish
by the assignment of certain tasks and then stick to the
main objective. Do not allow yourself to become side-
tracked. You want them to clean their bedroom, for

example, to teach them personal hygiene and responsibility, not to make you feel better because the room is tidy.

The U.S. Department of Health, Education, and Welfare pamphlet entitled *The Adolescent in Your Family* suggests that in training your teenager, your attitude toward him plays a greater part than any plan you devise. Children can pick up a grumbling, complaining attitude as well as a cheerful one in taking on the challenge of a difficult task. It may be helpful to write down the things you hate to do and have your teenager write down the chores he hates to do. Then compare the list and note how his likes and dislikes reflect your attitudes. The pamphlet further encourages parents to consider the value of a task and the aptitude required to perform it. Ask these questions:

1. Who cares about work just anyone can do?

2. Why am I asked to do this job?

3. Is it because no one else wants it or because they think I can do it especially well?

4. Am I being asked to do it because of my age, talents, etc?

Maybe your son, who has a sharp eye for bargaining, would do better at buying the family groceries than cleaning the basement.

Apply logical consequences and methods of discipline. I recently met a teenager who had the idea that hopping in the car any time he pleased to run errands was acceptable. This continued no matter now often he was reproached by his parents. Rather than create harder feelings, I suggested to the mother and father that they keep the keys to the car completely out of their son's reach. This forced him to ask permission to take the car. This, of course, was the desired outcome and reduced the conflict because the parents had greater control, which in turn led to more responsible behavior by their son. Applying logical consequences can be an important motivator.

Offer alternatives. Another way to help your adolescent develop independence is to offer alternatives. All your children need responsibility, but it need not be imposed on them. If together you and your teens discuss which chores are expected to be done, then choose which each person will do, the chores are more likely to be done. It is sometimes difficult to come up with alternative solutions to problems, especially if this has not been common practice in your family. The following exercise may be helpful. For each specific problem define at least two alternative solutions:

1. I hate my science teacher. I'm going to quit school.
   a. Transfer to another science class.
   b. Talk out the problem with the teacher you dislike.
2. I'm not going to the dance. I don't have anything to wear.
   a. Ask to borrow a sister's dress.
   b. Purchase material and make one of your own.
3. I can never please my father. I'm going to quit trying.
   a. Go to your father and talk about your discomfort.
   b. Think of ways to help Father rather than resisting him.

What problems do your teenagers face? Help them to formulate beneficial alternatives.

Like all of us, teenagers need to know that they are loved and appreciated. They need to be reassured of this over and over again. They need to feel that they are important and useful, that they are capable of making significant contributions. Helping your teenager toward independence has its moments of humor and pathos, joy and disappointment, challenge and satisfaction. But what a great feeling it is when they come back to say, "Thanks, Mom and Dad, for sticking by me and helping me make it."

Appropriate Age for Dating

34

Question

I have a fourteen-year-old daughter whom I believe is too young to begin dating. Unfortunately, she has developed physically much more rapidly than she has emotionally and seems to have developed an early interest in boys. She desperately wants to socialize with them, but I feel that she is too eager. Can you help me determine when an early developer should be ready to date and whether it's unwise socially to permit her to begin to develop relationships without some supervision?

Answer

In my opinion, parents have an obligation to delay serious unsupervised dating until a child is both physically and emotionally ready to handle the responsibility of such a relationship. I think a good starting age for dating is sixteen, and even then it should at first be dating in groups or doubles. This is only a rule of thumb, but I think it applies generally to both males and females. Experience has taught me that early dating usually leads to early intimacy and early commitment. In these circumstances, our children are forced to make decisions that have life-long consequences without the proper education, guidance, and training. Couples who date at an early age usually experience intimacy early and consequently are more vulnerable to early pregnancies. Aside from the question of sexual morality, this places the youth in a real dilemma: They're typically too young to marry, yet they feel some parental responsibility to have and rear the child, and may be further confused by social norms regarding abortion and/or adoption. (I should mention that I do not believe in abortion except in cases of incest or rape. I have found that many women experience life-long emotional consequences after undergoing an abortion.)

There are several issues you should take into account as you determine the appropriate time for your child to begin dating. First, consider the physiological and social maturity of the child. Some adolescents are not ready to date even at sixteen because for one reason or another they lack the experience in relationship building. For example, your child may be shy or withdrawn, experiencing difficulty in creating social contacts. To let him slip into a one-to-one dating relationship without the opportunity to develop a variety of social skills may be disastrous, even though he may be old enough to date.

Second, as parents we have an obligation to create structured social settings that allow our adolescents to experiment with relationships, to learn gradually how to get along in social settings. I recommend for those who develop early that they be provided opportunities to socialize and to cultivate mature social skills in a setting where there is plenty of adult supervision. At the same time, parents should observe their children to determine what skills they may need to work on in order to have positive dating experiences. For example, observation in such a setting may reveal that your child needs to become a better listener; practice can help him to develop these skills. If, on the other hand, your child seems to want to steal the show all the time and is attracting negative attention, you can point out the problem and show your child what to do in the social setting. Give him opportunities to practice as well.

My third suggestion has to do with group activities, which can be particularly useful in helping our children develop social skills in a safe environment. The safety of a group setting cannot be overstated. Within the confines of the group, our children learn how other people interact; they see models of appropriate and inappropriate behavior; and they can test their own social skills in the company of many different people. This provides a varied feedback which teaches children the best ways to get along with others. If our children have not experienced group activities it would be wise to make sure that they do before we allow them to begin individual dating.

A fourth consideration: Decide beforehand on appropriate dating behavior with your child. Tell him how men and women should treat each other. Talk about etiquette and dating protocol. Even though some of our feelings about dating may seem old-fashioned to our children, proper decorum and consideration are still most appropriate in a dating situation. Boys ought to understand how to treat a young woman with respect and dignity, and young ladies ought to understand how to demand respect from their male counterparts. Discuss how to interact, how to decide on an activity, and how to relate politely with one another. These discussions can deter many negative complications.

It is appropriate during the dating years that our children clearly understand male and female roles in sexual behavior. It's also important to discuss the role of intimacy in a relationship. I try to make it clear to the young people I talk to that, aside from the compelling religious and moral considerations against it, physical intimacy before marriage is destructive. Typically, early intimacy leads to guilt, anxiety, and usually the destruction rather than reinforcement of close relationships. Adolescents ought to be taught how to say no and how far to allow things to go.

In summary, if we as parents can relax to some degree and become a little more flexible in handling the dating of each of our children, we will find that with cooperation and careful planning, we can help our children move from childhood into adolescence and relationship-building with the least amount of stress. Much of the success that they will have in their courtship experience will depend on how good a model we are in our own relationships as husbands and wives, how much information we give them regarding their own drives and needs, how much opportunity they have for developing social skills, and the education they get regarding dating relationships and physical intimacy.

Whatever Happened to . . . ?

35

Whatever happened to:

Kids who always played with children much younger than themselves?

Kids who played only with older kids?

Kids who didn't know the meaning of clean and neat?

Kids who always hit?

Kids who always seemed just a little below average in school and who never seemed to mind?

Kids who never left their mother's side?

Kids who seemed to have their days and nights mixed up?

Kids who preferred to play with only kids of the opposite sex?

Kids who seemed to have a preoccupation with their private parts?

Kids who never seemed to mind anything or anyone?

Kids who were afraid of almost everything—sleeping without a light, the dark, being alone, going outside, death, fire, cold, flood?

Kids who were always tripping over things and were terribly uncoordinated?

Kids who were lefthanded?

Kids who seemed to be accident prone?

Kids who were always in trouble with the teacher?

Kids who never learned to do things after being told just once?

Kids who cleaned their rooms by stuffing everything under their bed?

Kids who tried smoking the cigars they found on the road?

Kids who seemed to be happy only when they were teasing or tattling or crying?

Kids who wet the bed?

Kids who sucked their thumbs?

Kids who twitched?

Kids who had a security blanket for eighteen years?

Kids who wouldn't hug?

Kids who had the insatiable need to take things apart but never to put them back together?

Kids who were always breaking bones?

Kids who asked question after question and never wanted an answer?

Kids who were sick a lot?

Kids who were always coughing but never seemed to have a cold?

Kids who took things from stores without paying for them?

Kids who actually liked Boo-Berry cereal?

Kids who never took baths, brushed their teeth, or washed their hair enough?

Kids who wouldn't take naps?

Boys who played with dolls?

Girls who hated dolls?

Well, they all grew up. Most got married, got jobs, and joined the human masses. Some became presidents of countries, corporations, and banks. Most became husbands/wives, mothers/fathers. And nearly all began to ask these same questions at about the age of thirty-five.

Index